WALKS IN THE WESTERN ISLES
Harris

pocket mountains

The author and publisher have made every effort to ensure that the information in this publication is accurate, and accept no responsibility whatsoever for any loss, injury or inconvenience experienced by any person or persons whilst using this book.

published by
pocket mountains ltd
The Old Church, Annanside,
Moffat, Dumfries & Galloway DG10 9HB
www.pocketmountains.com

ISBN: 978-1-907025-945

Text and photography copyright © Peter Edwards

The right of Peter Edwards to be identified as the Author of this work has been asserted by him in accordance with the Copyright, Designs and Patents Act 1988.

A catalogue record for this book is available from the British Library.
Contains Ordnance Survey data © Crown copyright and database 2023 supported by out of copyright mapping 1945-1961.

All rights reserved. No part of this publication may be reproduced, stored in a retrieval system, or transmitted in any form or by any means, electronic or mechanical, including photocopying and recording, unless expressly permitted by Pocket Mountains Ltd.

Printed by J Thomson Colour Printers, Glasgow

Introduction

At the heart of the Outer Hebrides island chain, the Isle of Harris – Na Hearadh – is known as a stronghold of the Gaelic language and of a distinctive traditional culture, where crofting and fishing remain fundamental to island life, fine quality Harris Tweed is still woven in small loom sheds and the Sabbath is still widely observed. Beyond the island's shores, however, Harris is perhaps best known for combining dazzling white sand beaches, sparkling turquoise waters and rugged heather-clad hinterlands to stunning effect. For many years this winning combination of landscape and island culture has provided the pull for visitors, undaunted by the island's meteorological reputation and the odd cloud of ferocious midges.

Lying some 50km from the mainland across The Minch, Harris – together with its semi-detached neighbour, Lewis – is the largest of the Scottish islands. Lewis comprises the larger northern part; both are frequently referred to as separate islands, principally because there is a geographical 'border' of sorts, formed by the mountainous boundary of the Harris Hills and the lengthy incursions of Loch Rèasort from the west and the fjord-like Loch Seaforth from the east.

Much of Harris is hilly, with more than 30 peaks at over 300m. The highest of these is The Clisham (An Cliseam), which at 799m is the highest mountain in the Outer Hebrides. Harris is also blessed with a remarkable coastline: the west coast is garlanded with dune-backed white sand beaches, while the rugged eastern coastline is punctuated with beautiful headlands, coves and bays.

This guidebook brings together 25 of the best walking routes, from strolls along the west coast's white sand beaches and half-day walks on rugged coastal paths to day-long mountain ridge traverses and wild country backpacking routes. Some of these routes are relatively popular, such as the walk to Eilean Glas Lighthouse on Scalpay and the Rhenigidale Postman's Path. Others are largely unfrequented, including An Coileach and Heileasbhal Mòr in South Harris and the Taran Mòr backpacking route through the northwest of the island.

As travel to the islands has become quicker and easier, so recent years have seen an increase in visitors from near and far as tourism continues to play an important part in the island economy. In the summer months the ferry port of Tarbert is abustle with visitors arriving and departing, cars and vans bristling with bikes, kayaks and surfboards, while brightly-hued campervans and pannier-laden touring cyclists dip in and out of the passing places along the sinuous single-track roads.

However, Harris remains very much a working landscape with crofting, creel boats and livestock farming still mainstays of island life while fish farms, a new marina, the Isle of Harris Distillery and a plethora of small enterprises add to the air of industry about the place.

Though together Lewis and Harris are the most populous of the Scottish islands, with around 21,000 permanent residents, Harris itself has a population of just 1900.

Weather

The Hebridean weather can be challenging – high winds and persistent rain are not uncommon but, contrary to popular myth, sunshine is also a frequent phenomenon in the Outer Hebrides. In fact, the Hebridean climate, greatly influenced by the North Atlantic Drift, is generally milder than the mainland. Island weather is also changeable, which usually provides some variety over the course of a few days, but you should be prepared and equipped for all eventualities when planning walks.

Access and safety

Public access to the countryside in Scotland is a statutory right. The Scottish Outdoor Access Code provides guidance both for those exercising their right to roam, and for land managers. See outdooraccess-scotland.scot.

Walkers have the right to roam over all open land, but this also comes with responsibilities. They must treat the environment and wildlife with care, respect the needs and privacy of those

Introduction

living and working in the countryside, not obstruct activities such as farming, crofting and deer stalking, and keep dogs under close control near livestock or ground-nesting birds. Sheep and cattle may be encountered roaming on roads, paths and beaches, so drive aware and be alert when walking with dogs.

Check weather forecasts before setting out and allow plenty of time to complete walks. Always let someone know your intended route and estimated time of completion. While some of the routes featured here follow clear paths and tracks — some signposted and waymarked, others not — others follow vague and intermittent paths at best, requiring a degree of navigational competence.

Getting there and getting around

Caledonian MacBrayne ferries sail from Uig, Skye to Tarbert, Harris and from the mainland port of Ullapool to Stornoway. Book well ahead for vehicles as the ferries can be very busy, especially in summer.

Loganair flies to Stornoway from Inverness, Edinburgh and Glasgow. Harris has a network of bus routes connecting most townships with Tarbert and Stornoway, hence many of these walks can be accessed by public transport — though timetables are often organised around schooldays.

If driving or cycling, familiarise yourself with the correct use of passing places on single-track roads, including letting vehicles overtake safely.

History

There are extensive traces of Neolithic culture in the Hebrides; the best-known site is the spectacular megalithic standing stones at Callanish (Calanais) in Lewis. Bronze Age sites are also found throughout the islands, including hut circles, field systems and burial cairns.

Viking raiders arrived in the islands at the end of the 8th century and formal Norse control followed in 1098. The Norsemen ruled the islands until 1156 when the Norse-Gael warlord Somerled took control of the Inner Hebrides, while the Outer Hebrides remained in Norse hands until they were ceded to the Kingdom of Scotland at the Treaty of Perth in 1266. Somerled's descendants, Clan Donald – known as the Lords of the Isles – emerged as the most important power in northwest Scotland, ruling the isles until 1493.

With the Treaty of Union in 1707, the Hebrides became part of the new Kingdom of Great Britain, although there was considerable support for the Stuart cause among the island clan chiefs during the 1715 and 1745 Jacobite rebellions. In 1746 the decisive defeat of Charles Edward Stuart's forces at the Battle of Culloden brought serious repercussions for the highlanders and islanders. The British government broke up the clan system and turned the Hebrides into a series of landed estates. The descendants of the clan chiefs became English-speaking landlords more concerned with revenues generated by their estates than the condition of those who lived on them. Rents were increased, Gaelic-speaking was discouraged and the wearing of folk dress was outlawed.

In the mid-19th century crofting communities were devastated by the Clearances. Throughout the Highlands and Islands populations were evicted – often forcibly – and replaced with sheep and deer. In Harris, crofting communities were uprooted from the fertile machair of the west and transplanted to the poor soils of the east. Large-scale emigration followed, some voluntary, some forced, with islanders relocated to the west coast and Lowlands of mainland Scotland and the North American colonies.

The outlook for the depleted island communities remained bleak until rent strikes and land raids led to the passing of the 1886 Crofters Act. The Act set fair rents and guaranteed security of tenure and the right to bequeath crofts to a successor. Nonetheless, emigration from the Hebrides continued apace, and many communities dwindled through much of the 20th century. For those who remained, the economic situation gradually improved with cattle farming, fisheries and tourism providing much of the stimulus. The fortunes of islanders were also influenced by the lairds, landowners and entrepreneurs who owned much of the archipelago. The philanthropic entrepreneur, Lord Leverhulme, invested in infrastructure and economic development on Lewis and Harris – with limited success.

The population decline affecting the Hebrides since the mid-19th century has stalled to some extent in recent years, although high levels of unemployment and significantly lower incomes than the UK average persist, hence many young people still leave the islands for further education or employment and most don't return. This in turn has resulted in an ageing population.

Today the island economy is largely dependent on the public sector – with many jobs in healthcare and local government, including education and services. Farming, crofting, aquaculture, fishing and tourism also remain important sectors with the development of renewable energy – wind and wave power projects – a significant element of the future island economy. The impetus for local control of natural assets is part of a bigger picture for the future of the island communities, with the continuing movement towards community land ownership in the Western Isles.

Natural history

The Outer Hebrides are largely comprised of Lewisian gneisses, some of the oldest rocks in Europe. The rugged landscape of present-day Harris dates from the most recent glacial period of the Quaternary ice age when much of the rocky low-lying terrain was heavily scoured by the advancing ice sheet, creating the characteristic 'cnoc-and-lochan' topography of hillocks and small lochs. Sea levels rose as the glaciers melted, resulting in the archipelago of islands, skerries and reefs recognisable today. Vast quantities of sand and gravel deposited into the sea by glacial meltwaters were swept ashore by wind and wave action, forming the white sand beaches and sand dunes characteristic of the low-lying areas of the western coastline.

There are few native mammal species on the Outer Hebrides, but the chances of enjoying some wildlife encounters while out walking are good. Red deer haunt the crags and glens and are often seen when out walking, particularly in North Harris. Mountain hares are generally much more difficult to see and the local population on Harris is small. They tend to be solitary and are often found high up in the mountains. Otters have territories around much of the island's coastline and are most often seen around the rocky inlets and headlands of east Harris.

Common and Atlantic grey seals are abundant and are frequently seen basking on offshore rocks and skerries or observing onshore activity from the sea. Dolphins and porpoises can also be seen – particularly in the sea lochs and bays of east Harris – usually in the spring and summer months.

Few sights are as rewarding as a golden eagle soaring past a mountain ridge or effortlessly rising on thermals, except perhaps that of a white-tailed eagle flapping its barn door-sized wings as it patrols the coastline in search of prey. There is a good chance of spotting eagles if you spend a reasonable amount of time outdoors on Harris.

Eagles aside, the birdlife of the Outer Hebrides is rich, diverse and often spectacular. A number of rare and uncommon species, native and migrant, such as the corncrake, red-necked phalarope and great northern diver, are present in the islands, as are several of the most photogenic species, including the raven, gannet and puffin. See western-isles-wildlife.com for information on recent sightings.

Tòdun seen from the Urgha to Rhenigidale path

Contents

		page
1.	Rodel, Renish Point and St Clement's Church	13
2.	Roineabhal from Rodel	17
3.	Ceapabhal and the Temple	21
4.	An Coileach and Heileasbhal Mòr	27
5.	The Scholars' Path	33
6.	The Coffin Route	39
7.	Tràigh Sheileboist	45
8.	Beinn Dhubh and Luskentyre	49
9.	Tràigh Losgaintir	55
10.	The Skeaudale Horseshoe	59
11.	Scalpay and Eilean Glas	65
12.	Urgha to Rhenigidale on the Postman's Path	71
13.	Stràthabhal, An Reithe and Tòdun	79
14.	Rhenigidale and Loch Seaforth	85
15.	The Clisham Horseshoe	91
16.	The Glens of North Harris	99
17.	Stulabhal, Tèileasbhal and Uisgneabhal Mòr	105
18.	Muladal, Ulabhal, Oireabhal and Cleiseabhal	111
19.	Loch Chliostair and Gleann Uladail	115
20.	Harris Hills and Loch Rèasort backpack	121
21.	Tiorga Mòr	129
22.	Huiseabhal Mòr, Oireabhal and Crabhadail	133
23.	Hushinish and Crabhadail	139
24.	Crabhadail and Taran Mòr backpack	145
25.	St Kilda: walks on Hirta	153

Harris

St Clement's Church

Rodel, Renish Point and St Clement's Church

Distance 8km **Total ascent** 300m
Time 2 hours 30 **Terrain** minor roads, grassy paths, boggy in places along Renish Point **Map** OS Explorer 455 **Access** bus (W10) to Rodel from Leverburgh or Tarbert. If driving, park alongside the church wall near to the public toilets

Renish Point is the most southerly headland on Harris. A walk out to the modest high point (50m) near its southern extremity is rewarded with views along the coast, out across the island-dotted Sound of Harris and northwards to the rock-encrusted summit of Roineabhal rising above the settlement of Rodel. The splendid 16th-century St Clement's Church is very much worth a visit at the end of your walk.

The route benefits from an actual path for some of the way, though the walk along Renish Point crosses sheep grazing croftland, which can be muddy in places and requires dogs to be kept on a lead.

From St Clement's Church follow the road west past one turning and then take the next turn on your left, signed – in Gaelic and English – for Borrisdale. Shortly after crossing the bridge over the outflow of the loch, leave the road at the bend through a gate and follow the path straight ahead with views across to Renish Point. Keep to the main path as it contours above Loch Roghadail, soon climbing alongside a fence to reach a gate. Go through and continue as the path contours above the headland of Stuaidh and the inlet of Borosdale Bay.

Go through a gate and descend around the head of the inlet before climbing the other side to go through another gate. At the top, turn left onto a track and take this to the road end. Turn right to follow the road past a number of houses, then turn left at the first road junction and follow this to the road end where there is a parking area below a house overlooking the bay.

Turn right, go through a gate and follow the grassy track uphill to a sheep fank at the top. Go through a gate at the left of the fank and continue straight ahead, passing through two more stock gates. Once through the last gate, where the ground can be boggy, turn left along the fenceline to gain drier ground. Continue along the east side of the headland until you reach another fence, go through the gate and follow the sheep paths up towards the cairn-marked high point (50m), avoiding the boggy ground where you can.

Rodel, Renish Point and St Clement's Church

Though a modest height, the views are well worth the walk. Looking back to the north, Roineabhal looms large over Rodel with the tower of St Clement's above Loch Roghadail. To the southwest, a flotilla of small islands are scattered across the Sound of Harris, with the islands of Berneray, North Uist and South Uist beyond and Skye to the southeast. It's worth continuing down to the point for the potential wildlife-spotting opportunities – otters, porpoises and dolphins can be seen with patience and a bit of luck. It is also possible to explore the west coast of the headland as an alternative return route, but the outward route is the drier option.

Returning to Rodel, it's well worth taking some time for a good look around the church and graveyard of St Clement's; make sure you also climb up into the tower.

Dating from the early 16th century and imposingly situated atop a rocky outcrop, St Clement's was the traditional burial place of the chiefs of the MacLeods of Dunvegan. The interior of the church houses a number of wall tombs and grave slabs judged the finest late-medieval sculpture surviving in the Western Isles. The intricate carvings depict various religious themes and scenes reflecting the status of those commemorated. Of a somewhat less pious nature are the stone carvings set into the exterior of the tower depicting a man and woman exposing their genitals. Rather than being elaborate medieval graffiti, they are, in fact, what are known as Sheela-na-gig, examples of which can be found on early churches right across Europe. Various theories suggest that they may have served to warn against immorality, or that they might have been fertility symbols.

Harris

Looking north from above Coire Ròineabhail

Roineabhal from Rodel

Distance 8km **Total ascent** 490m
Time 3 hours 30 **Terrain** pathless, rugged terrain with expanses of bare rock and heather cover
Map OS Explorer 455 **Access** bus (W10) to Rodel from Leverburgh or Tarbert. If driving, park alongside the church wall near to the public toilets

A huge barnacled, whale-backed mountain, the rock-strewn bulk of Roineabhal dominates the landscape at Harris' southern extremity, rising above the township of Leverburgh and the settlement of Rodel (Roghadal).

Roineabhal looms large as visitors arrive at Leverburgh from Berneray on the Sound of Harris ferry, yet paradoxically this is a hill largely overlooked by walkers drawn to the more assertive peaks and elegant ridges of the Harris Hills further north. Even on a fine summer's day, you'll likely have the summit to yourself.

Admittedly, the mountain's rocky, barren-looking countenance may have something to do with this, so too the lack of obvious paths – in Old Norse, Roineabhal means 'Rough Hill' and this is an entirely apposite description. However, once you are clear of the rougher terrain lower down the mountain's flank, the walk out along the summit ridge is quite splendid with some truly sublime, expansive views. In spring and summer, there is the added bonus of numerous wildflowers, mosses and lichens adorning the mountain's rough pelt.

There are no footpaths to the summit marked on the map, but the usual ascent from Rodel follows the northern shore of Loch Thorsageàrraidh and then the upper reaches of the Abhainn Thorro to the summit. The route described here climbs the southeast ridge of Beinn na h-Àire and descends via the direct route to form a circular walk – alternatively you can simply retrace the outward route. The walk starts from the medieval St Clement's Church in Rodel – make sure you allow plenty of time for a good look round this fascinating church and its graveyard.

Head east along the A859, soon

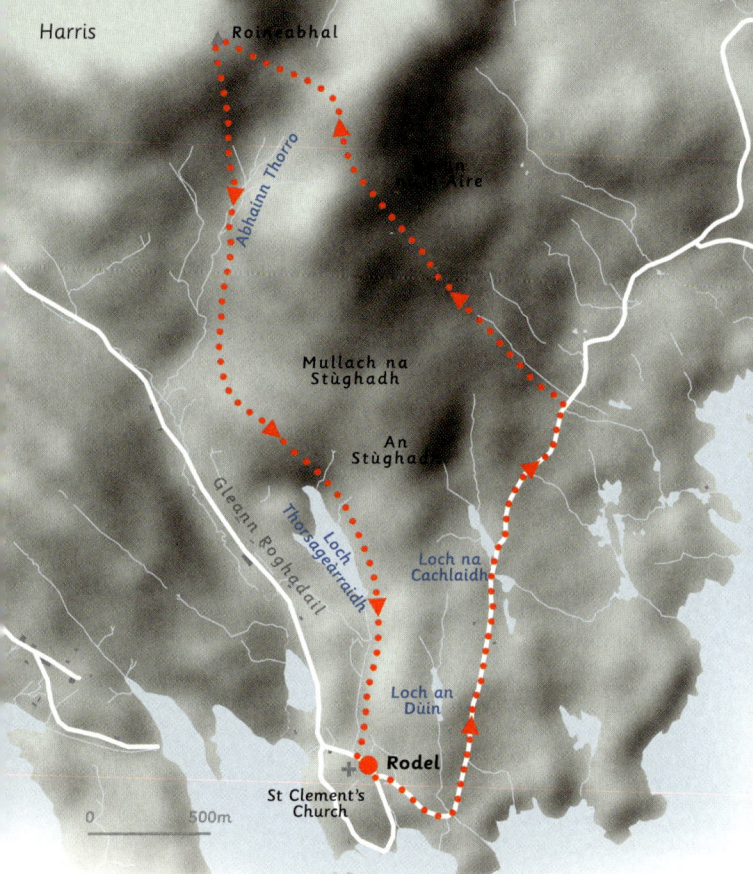

bearing left along the C79 road signposted for Fionnsabhagh (Finsbay). Follow the road, which soon turns northwards, for 2km, passing a radio mast and Loch na Cachlaidh before arriving atop a small hill (NG056846) marked with a spot height of 63m on the OS Explorer map. Leave the road here

Roineabhal from Rodel

and, keeping left of a burn, climb directly towards the lowest point in the ridge north of the cairn-marked southern summit of Beinn na h-Àire – 'the Hill of the Lookout'. The hillside can be wet in its lower reaches, but it becomes drier as you gain height. As you climb, the view opens up to take in the townships of The Bays to the northeast and the mountainous profile of Skye across The Minch to the southeast.

The gradient eases as you approach the ridge – bear north and make for the higher of Beinn na h-Àire's summits (398m) with its prominent cairn (NG047858). On a clear day, there are grand views southwest across the flotilla of islets and skerries in the Sound of Harris to Berneray and the hills of North and South Uist. A small cairn marks the way WNW across the bealach at the head of the dramatic caldera of Coire Ròineabhail, forming the sheer northern flank of the mountain. Continue WNW, climbing steadily up the scree and rock-strewn slope and passing a prominent cairn atop an outcrop immediately before the 460m-high summit of Roineabhal, which is furnished with a trig point surrounded by a stone shelter wall (NG042860). Two cairns adorn the northern side of the summit plateau, overlooking the verdant pastures of Rodel to the south, the loch-fringed township of Leverburgh to the west and the Harris Hills to the north.

When you can tear yourself away from the views, descend initially southwards from the summit, bearing southeast to pass below the rocky slopes of Beinn na h-Àire, noting the occasional small cairns marking the usual route of ascent. Resist descending too quickly and stay with the easier ground immediately below the rocks of Mullach na Stùghadh before dropping down to the north end of Loch Thorsageàrraidh. Pick up a grassy path heading southwards along its eastern shore. Keep heading south beyond the outflow of the loch, continuing through a dip fringed with gorse bushes as the church comes back into view ahead. On meeting a drystane dyke, follow it around to the left, eventually emerging at the road opposite the church.

Looking across Tràigh na Cleabhaig to Ceapabhal

Ceapabhal and the Temple

Distance 8km **Total ascent** 445m
Time 3 hours 30 **Terrain** tracks through machair and dunes, beaches, rough hill and moorland **Map** OS Explorer 455 **Access** bus (W10A) to Northton from Tarbert and Rodel

The humpbacked summit of Ceapabhal – 'the Bow-shaped Hill' in Old Norse – rises at the head of the narrow isthmus connecting it to the settlement of Northton at the southwest corner of Harris.

Approaching Northton by road, Ceapabhal rises to the west of the sandy sweep of Tràigh Scarasta, fringed by saltmarsh and separated on its eastern side by tidal sandflats. It makes for an impressive scene. No less spectacular are the panoramic views from the summit of Ceapabhal, encompassing the beaches and hills of south and west Harris, Taransay and the flotilla of islands scattered across the Sound of Harris.

The obvious and most-frequented route to the summit of Ceapabhal follows the tracks across the dunes and machair of the isthmus before launching directly up the steep southeast flank of the hill. Apart from being direct, there is little to recommend this route. Far better to take a slightly longer but more enjoyable route via the beach-fringed west side of the isthmus, visiting the splendidly-situated ruins of the ancient chapel, known as the Temple, at Rubha an Teampaill. There's no avoiding a stiff climb to get to the top of Ceapabhal, but the ensuing ascent via the southwest flank provides variety before descending by the direct route.

Park either at the Temple Café (please ask permission) or carefully near the road end past the turning circle or above the beach at Tràigh na h-Uidhe. Go through the gate at the road end to join the track across the machair – keep dogs on a lead as sheep and cattle are grazed here. After 100m or so, bear left off the path and head across the grazing pasture to a path running along the fenceline above the coast. Turn right to soon pass through lazy beds sloping down to the rocky shore. Continue through a gate with the lovely beach at

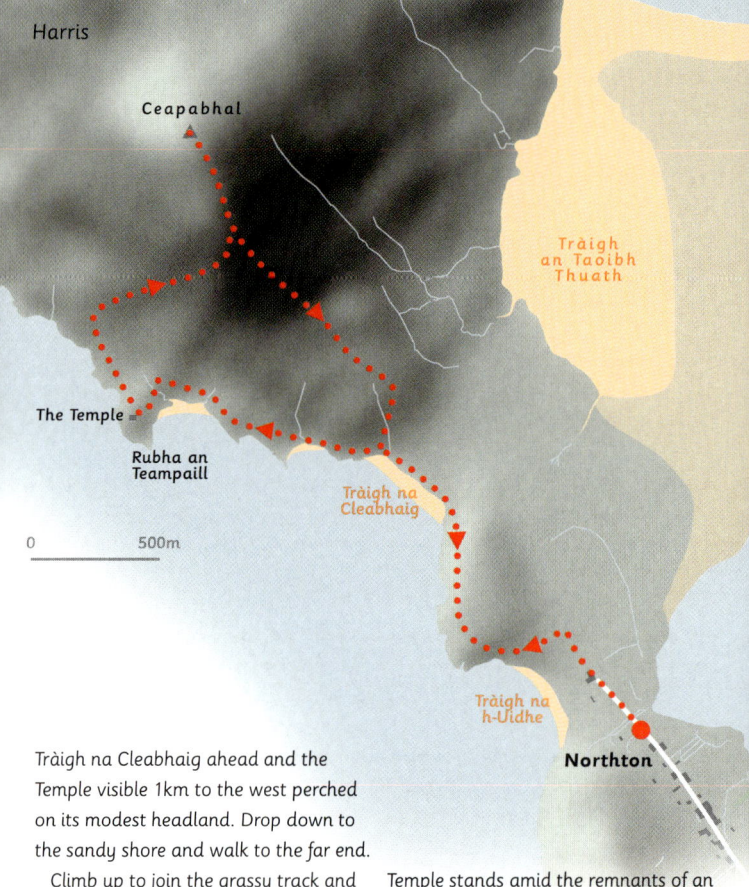

Tràigh na Cleabhaig ahead and the Temple visible 1km to the west perched on its modest headland. Drop down to the sandy shore and walk to the far end.

Climb up to join the grassy track and continue westwards to Rubha an Teampaill, passing or crossing another fine sandy beach en route.

A chapel built in the 16th century, the Temple stands amid the remnants of an older dun – or fortification – which likely supplied much of the stone used to build it. The Temple dates to 1528, built the same year as St Clement's Church at

Ceapabhal and the Temple

Rodel by Alasdair Crotach, Chief of the MacLeods. For a time, the Temple served as the parish church for the whole of Harris and the formerly populous islands of Pabbay and Berneray in the Sound of Harris, before eventually falling into disuse and disrepair.

From the Temple, follow the grassy track northwest towards a drystane dyke and cross this wherever easiest. Head northwards uphill to the rock outcrops forming part of the band of exposed rock climbing the hillside obliquely north to south. There is a vague mossy path to follow around the top edge of the rocks until you reach a small boulderfield, which the path works its way beneath before continuing to climb around the hillside. The path eventually clears the rocky terrain and becomes more distinct as you climb, joining the main up-and-down path once you reach the southeast flank.

Follow the path up to an OS trig point and on to a stone pile cairn a short distance beyond, which is the summit proper at 368m. On a clear day the views are immense: to the northeast beyond the beach-garlanded west coast and the island of Taransay stands the phalanx of Harris Hills. To the south, Pabbay, Ensay, Killegray, Berneray and a collection of smaller islets lie scattered across the Sound of Harris with North Uist beyond. Depending on visibility, the islands and sea stacks of the St Kilda archipelago may also be seen 80km away to the west.

Once you've absorbed the views, head back down the main path, which is quite easy to follow if a little steep in places. The view back across the sand-fringed isthmus to Northton and the surrounding hills is also quite breathtaking. Continue straight down the path to a fence, which you can cross via a step stile and return directly along the track to Northton or, better still, turn right along the fenceline and follow it down to a gate at the corner of a drystane dyke above the shore. The latter option takes you back the way you came via the beaches and coast to Northton, following the path through the gate above the southern end of Tràigh na Cleabhaig.

Descending the southeast ridge of Ceapabhal

Ceapabhal and the Temple

Descending northwards from the summit of Heileasbhal Mòr

An Coileach and Heileasbhal Mòr

Distance 10.5km **Total ascent** 645m
Time 5 hours **Terrain** pathless, rugged, rough and rocky hillcountry, boggy in places **Map** OS Explorer 455
Access bus (W13) to Seilebost from Tarbert and Leverburgh

The line of rocky hills forming the gnarled spine of South Harris is largely overlooked by walkers, perhaps in part because of its proximity to the astonishingly beautiful sands at Seilebost and Luskentyre, but certainly also because it inhabits a domain of rough, rocky, boggy and pathless terrain.

When setting off to climb the central summits of An Coileach and Heileasbhal Mòr, it's easy to see why speculative walkers might be put off, but these are hills very much worth persevering for. Once on the high ground this is a walk full of interest and some absolutely sensational views – if you have clear conditions.

That said, this is neither a walk for inexperienced hillwalkers – the terrain is complex and navigational competence is required – nor those with an aversion to very rough and potentially boggy terrain. Nor is this a walk for anything other than fine weather – ideally with good visibility – and preferably undertaken during a dry spell to minimise the boggy factor.

Around 1.5km beyond the Losgaintir turning (travelling westwards from Tarbert), take the left-hand turn by the Seilebost roadsign just beyond the end of the causeway. Continue past a couple of houses to a water pumping station with a red roof – there is space for parking opposite.

Go through a metal stock gate to the left of the pumping station and continue up the initially rocky track along the left bank of the Abhainn Gil an Tàilleir. The broad track is often very muddy as you progress up towards another pumping station. After passing a concrete sluice gate in the river, continue following the course of the burn while trying to remain dry shod, which may require moving away from the burn at times. The going is intermittently wet and spongy.

To your left (southeast), the long ridge of Maoladh Mhicearraig climbs up towards the summit of Ceann Reamhar na Sròine, to the southwest the long rocky ridge of Heileasbhal Mòr. Ahead lies the as yet undistinguished hump of Clunaisbhal, with An Coileach not yet visible. Once the foot of the ridge is in striking distance, cross the burn – with care – and head up onto its rough flank. The gradient soon becomes steady with rock bands and outcrops making for easier progress. The Lewisian gneiss is gritty and good for friction.

After climbing at length, the crenellated crest of the hill comes into view. Pass around a small lochan beneath the rocky outcrop and gain the right flank of this outcrop where it's easiest to ascend – the view back to Taransay, Luskentyre and the Harris Hills is tremendous. Once on the outcrop, which is the summit proper (389m), continue southwards to the OS trig point at the slightly lower end of the summit ridge. There are stunning views eastwards over The Bays of Harris with Skye across The Minch and southwest to the whale-backed form of Roineabhal.

Retrace your steps a short way, then head northwestwards, descending through a heathery declivity between rocky slabs to arrive near the southern end of a long unnamed lochan in the Bealach na Ciste. Head up the eastern flank of Heileasbhal Mòr, initially following a band of gneiss obliquely uphill. The gneiss bears some incredible sworls and folds caused by buckling under extreme heat and pressure during formation. The cairn-marked summit (384m) comes into view and once you actually get there it makes for a great vantage point with views of Roineabhal and the islands of the Sound of Harris beyond. To the north lies the undistinguished hump of Carran, the next and final summit on the itinerary.

From the summit, head northwards through rugged, lochan-scattered

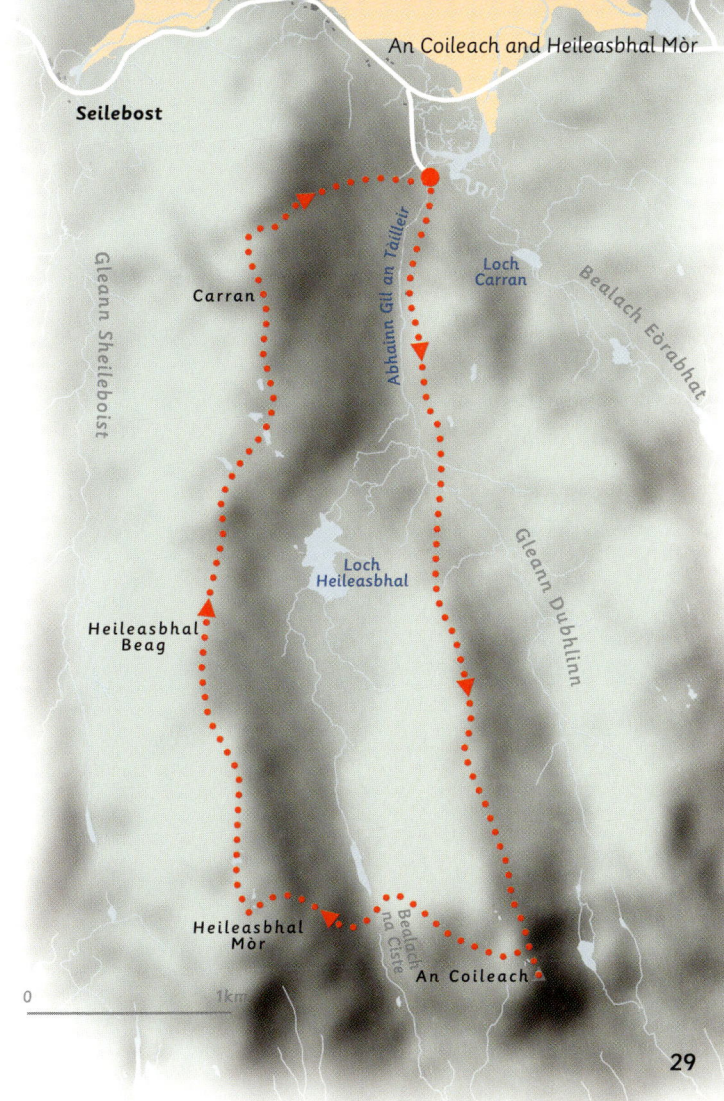

Harris

terrain with fine views of Taransay ahead. Continue descending over Heileasbhal Beag to a bealach with a brown smudge where Loch Heileasbhal used to be below to your right. Continue across the bealach, being wary of boggy ground, and begin the long and convoluted ascent of Carran. Steer a course around lochans, across small ridges and through declivities at what seems great length until finally a series of cairns mark the vicinity of the summit (245m). Continue to the most northeasterly of the cairns, which has the most remarkable outlook over the sands of Luskentyre and Seilebost with Taransay and the Harris Hills completing the extraordinary picture.

Looking across Tràigh Losgaintir from the flank of Carran

An Coileach and Heileasbhal Mòr

On the Scholars' Path by the Allt Steinis

The Scholars' Path

Distance 9.5km **Total ascent** 350m
Time 3 hours **Terrain** metalled, well-drained grassy path, some wet ground, minor road **Map** OS Explorer 455
Access bus (W13) to Ardvey junction from Tarbert and Leverburgh. Parking, with care, next to the recycling point by the Lackalee (Leac a Lì) turning at the head of Loch Stocanais

Before the Golden Road – so called because of the construction cost – was built to connect the scattered townships of the Bays of Harris in the 1940s, the 'Scholars' Path' was used by children to get to school at Grosebay (Greòsabhagh), then subsequently at Kyles Stockinish (Caolas Stocinis) when a school was built there.

The path was built in the late 1890s with support from the authentically Victorian-sounding Congested Districts Board, which suggests the population of the Bays was then deemed greater than the land could support. The route of the path was ingeniously thought out, working with the terrain rather than against it and it was also evidently very well constructed as it is still in good condition today, generally well-drained, even underfoot, and a pleasure to walk on. There are great views and a number of interesting ruins on the route to keep the interest piqued.

There are various options for walking the Scholars' Path. It can be walked one-way in either direction from Lackalee or Grosebay if you arrange transport or make cunning use of the bus service. It can also be walked out and back as it's not a particularly long path and you get to enjoy the views in both directions.

The route described here starts at the T-junction by Lackalee and follows the path to Grosebay. The return retraces the outward route as far as Loch an Rothaid, then takes to the low stone-capped ridge of Càrnan Mòr, following a trail of cairns back to the start with fine views along the way.

From the T-junction at the north end of Lackalee, follow the road northeast for 300m to a sign on the right for Stocanais and Greòsabhagh. Head up through a metal gate and bear left

33

Harris

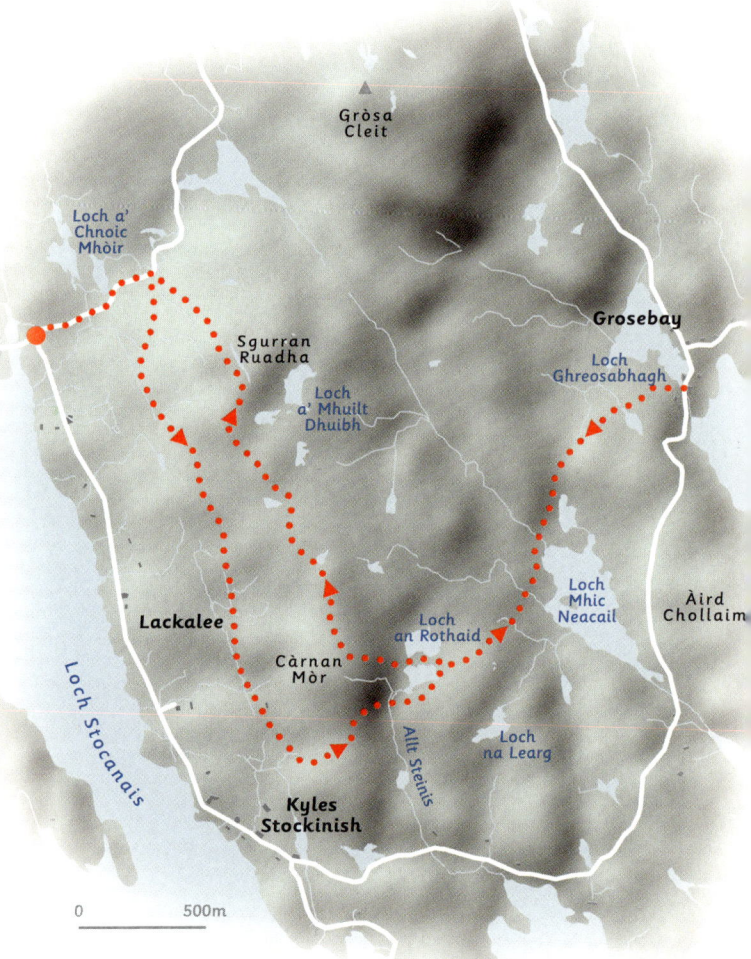

(marker post with blue band), climbing with the fenceline towards a wooden gate. Don't go through this but instead bear right, following the fence and marker posts. After 300m, go through a gate in the fences on the left and continue southwards along the path with its regular marker posts and occasional gates.

Carry on along a gentle downhill section of path with fine views out along Loch Stocanais where a surprising small roofless ruin appears on the right with a stone pile cairn nearby. The diminutive structure incorporates a very large boulder into its rear end, adding to the overall oddness. Perhaps it was a shelter for the path's scholars at one time. Continue through another gate and a gap in a tumbledown drystane dyke before the path descends through a gap between rocky outcrops. The impressive stone-built remains of a large blackhouse with a burn running past stands just below the path. A little further on, the roofless remains of a large derelict chapel sit above the path. Carry on to where a three-way signpost stands next to a gate above Kyles Stockinish; turn left here for Greòsabhagh, heading up a slight rise to pass through a pair of gates by a drystane-walled enclosure.

The path climbs a little further, passes through another gate and then swoops down in a sinuous bend to cross the Allt Steinis flowing down from Loch an Rothaid and under the path by means of twin culverts capped with stone slabs. Now the path climbs a little, levels and continues on its way to Loch Mhic Neacail. Before the path drops to follow the western edge of the loch, a thoughtfully placed bench perches on high with a fine outlook over the water. Cross a stone bridge, then a wooden footbridge and the path soon descends to Grosebay, passing a haulage and public transport vehicle graveyard and traversing a boggy section before passing through a gate to reach the road.

From Grosebay, retrace the outward route for around 1.5km. At a bend leave the path to head westwards along the isthmus between the twin lochs at Loch an Rothaid. Step over the burn flowing between the upper and lower lochs. There are some boggy patches to avoid between the outcrops of slabby rock, but the going is generally good as you climb westwards to the cairn-marked summit of Càrnan Mòr (110m). The views of the Bays of Harris from the top of this modest hill are a theme that continues as you head northwestwards along the stone-capped ridge, following a regular series of little cairns winding through the lochan-dotted terrain.

After 1.5km pass to the left of a long narrow lochan and descend along the rocky ridge running parallel to a stock fence below to the left. Continue downhill, following the fence to reach the road a short way from the signpost at the start of the Scholars' Path. Turn left to follow the road back to the T-junction.

Unusual small ruin on the Scholars' Path

The Scholars' Path

Harris

The Coffin Route

Distance 14km **Total ascent** 380m
Time 5 hours **Terrain** waymarked moorland paths and tracks, returning on old road and stretches beside the main road **Map** OS Explorer 455 **Access** bus (W13) to Ardvey junction from Tarbert and Leverburgh. Parking, with care, next to the recycling point by the Lackalee (Leac a Li) turning at the head of Loch Stocanais

The Coffin Route is the path formerly used to carry the dead from the Bays of Harris on the rugged, rocky east coast – with its sparse covering of wet, peaty soil – over the spine of the island to the silver sands and machair of the west coast where the deeper, better-drained soils are better suited for burial.

Latterly, the path has become a well-established, comprehensively waymarked walking route that co-opts stretches of other paths, old roads and newer roads to make a circular route from east coast to west coast and back again. Together with its historical

Looking northwest to Seilebost and Taransay from the Coffin Route

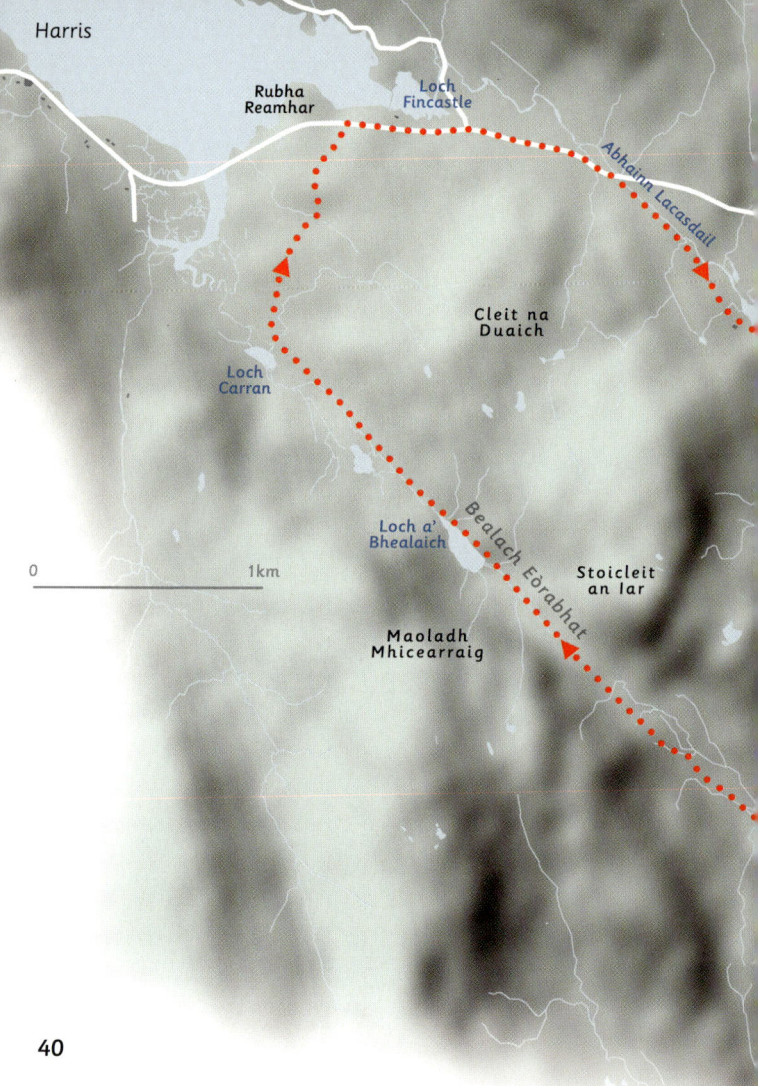

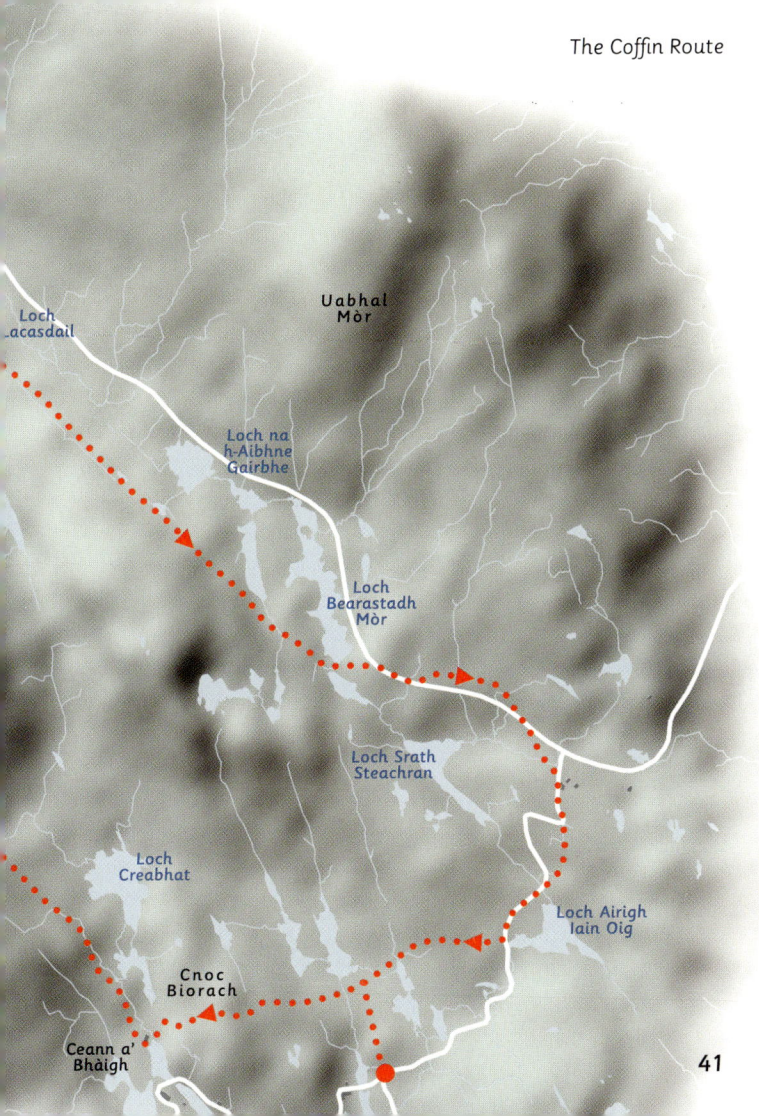

interest, this walk has some great views – especially westwards from the Bealach Eòrabhat – as well as flora, fauna and plenty of gnarly Lewisian gneiss to look out for along the way.

The Coffin Route starts from the T-junction at the northern end of Lackalee (Leac a Lì) at the head of Loch Stocanais in the Bays of Harris. There is parking space by the recycling bins next to the start of the path, which is signposted Gu Losgaintir (An Taobh Siar), To Luskentyre (West Side). There are marker posts (blue bands near the top) dotted along the route with varying frequency.

The beginning of the route is an old stretch of road, though this soon runs out at a sheep fank. Go through a gate on the left side of the fank and continue to a T-junction with another path at a three-way signpost. Turn left (signed for Ceann a' Bay and Seilebost), cross a footbridge and continue straight ahead beneath Cnoc Biorach, ignoring a stile over a fence on the left. The path continues alongside the fence before descending in a zigzag and following another fence down to a metal gate near a house at Ceann a Bhàigh. Go through, cross a bridge and turn right – a signpost indicates Seilebost – passing a large detached garage. This next section of the walk follows the course of the old Coffin Route.

As you carry on, the path begins to climb gently, soon passing Loch Creabhat below to the east. The path, which was once notoriously boggy in places, has been improved in recent years with drainage channels and gravel. The path heads up through rough terrain as the way narrows between the craggy heights of Maoladh Mhicearraig to the west and Stoicleit an Iar to the east – this is golden eagle country, so keep an eye to the sky as you climb. The gradient eases as you approach the Bealach Eòrabhat, finally levelling out before the path begins its westward descent with the view down to Tràigh Losgaintir and out across the sound to Taransay opening up.

The path gives way to a gravel track running downhill past Loch a' Bhealaich and eventually reaches a T-junction with an old disused section of road by Loch Carran. Go through the gate, then turn right through another gate and follow the old road with views across the sands before arriving at another gate leading down onto the A859. Turn right and continue along the verge with care. Pass the turning signed for Losgaintir on the left, then after a further 600m turn right onto the old road signed for Laxdale Cottage. The old road leads past the cottage by Loch Lacasdail and continues climbing steadily, passing a series of lochans. The old road then passes through a working quarry, so observe the cautions on the warning signs. If a siren is sounded, wait for an all clear before proceeding.

Shortly after the quarry, the old road rejoins the A859. Turn right along the verge for a short way before forking left to follow a shorter stretch of the old road. Rejoin the A859 briefly before forking right onto yet another section of the old road that cuts the corner to join the minor road leading down to Lackalee and the starting point. At the first bend, you can bear left off the road to follow a grassy path to cut across to the next bend. After a further 300m, you can turn right off the road at a passing place opposite Loch Airigh Iain Oig and follow the grassy path down to a path junction, turning left to pass the fank and return to the start. Otherwise just follow the road.

Tràigh Sheileboist

Distance 3.5km **Total ascent** 50m
Time 1 hour 30 **Terrain** sandy beach, dunes, track **Map** OS Explorer 455
Access bus (W10) to Seilebost from Tarbert and Leverburgh

Jutting northwards from the southern edge of the vast tidal sandflats of Tràigh Losgaintir, the shark's tooth-shaped, dune-fringed spit of land known as Corran Sheileboist pointedly makes the case for spending some time exploring the surrounding sandflats and the splendid beach of Tràigh Sheileboist at its western edge.

Though it's also a very beautiful spot, Tràigh Sheileboist gets fewer visitors than Tràigh Losgaintir; it also enjoys fine views across the sandflats to its illustrious neighbour with the summits of Beinn Dhubh and Beinn Losgaintir rising above the settlement strung out along the single-track road.

From the A859 road, walk or drive down the track signed for the Sgoil Sheileboist – there is an obvious parking area opposite the school building. Head north along the grassy path towards the dunes. From here, you can wander at your leisure, though you could head out through the dunes and drop down to the sandflats on the eastern, inland side, head out onto the sandflats with care as the tide allows and return along the magnificent sandy strand of Tràigh Sheileboist, enjoying views across to the island of Taransay, before cutting back through the dunes at a convenient point on the way back to your starting point.

Harris

Tràigh Sheileboist

Looking along Tràigh Sheileboist with Ceapabhal in the distance

Looking across Tràigh Losgaintir from the flank of Sròn Godamuil

Beinn Dhubh and Luskentyre

Distance 11.5km **Total ascent** 600m
Time 4 hours 30 **Terrain** largely pathless hill and moorland terrain, avoidable easy scrambling over slabs; boggy ground; a steep and occasionally rough descent from Beinn Losgaintir
Map OS Explorer 455 **Access** bus (W13) to Luskentyre turning (request stop) from Tarbert and Leverburgh

Beinn Dhubh and its whale-backed ridge of contiguous hills rise up between West Loch Tarbert and the Sound of Taransay, providing the best vantage point in all of Harris.

The Harris Hills lie to the north, the island of Taransay to the west and the turquoise waters and silver sands of Tràigh Losgaintir immediately below to the southwest. It's this commanding position which really provides the walk with its crowning glory, but it is also an enjoyable and not excessively taxing hillwalking route in its own right with a visit to the sands of Tràigh Rosamol – and Tràigh Losgaintir if you're inclined – included on the return.

From the junction with the A859, head along the Luskentyre road for 400m (you can park carefully a short way to the west along a wide stretch of road). Go through the kissing gate next to another iron gate on the north side of the Losgaintir road and cross the Allt Totain 'ic Fannan on stones a short way upstream. Making for the rocky spur of Sròn Godamuil, cross some initially very boggy ground to reach the foot of the slabs. These can be scrambled up without difficulty or largely avoided by keeping left and weaving a route through the slabs. The gradient soon eases and the terrain becomes drier, making for a more enjoyable ascent.

Make for the summit of Sròn Godamuil, marked with two small cairns; from here, pass a small lochan and continue ascending steadily northwards, with the terrain becoming less rocky as you climb. As you reach the broad ridge at Mullach Buidhe, marked by a small cairn, the view opens up to the Harris Hills to the north. Continue northwest along the broad ridge that makes for easy walking to the summit of Beinn Losgaintir (436m),

Harris

which is marked with a more substantial cairn. The views across West Loch Tarbert to the Harris Hills are by now fairly sensational while southwest the view stretches along the coast well beyond Tràigh Losgaintir.

Descend a short way towards an unnamed lochan in the bealach, then make the 100m climb up the broad slope to gain the summit of Beinn Dhubh, marked with a trig point surrounded by a stone shelter wall. On a clear day, you'll need a handbook of superlatives to do justice to the views, with Taransay and the vast Atlantic Ocean hogging the limelight to the west. From the summit, continue WNW to reach a couple of cairns marking the end of the ridge. The ground falls away steeply, so initially bear west to descend grassy, boulder-strewn ground that gives way to a broad heathery slope as it steepens. Where the gradient eventually eases, head towards the pebble bay at Mol an Tighe at the foot of the Abhainn Àird Grothadnais but go through a gate in the fence

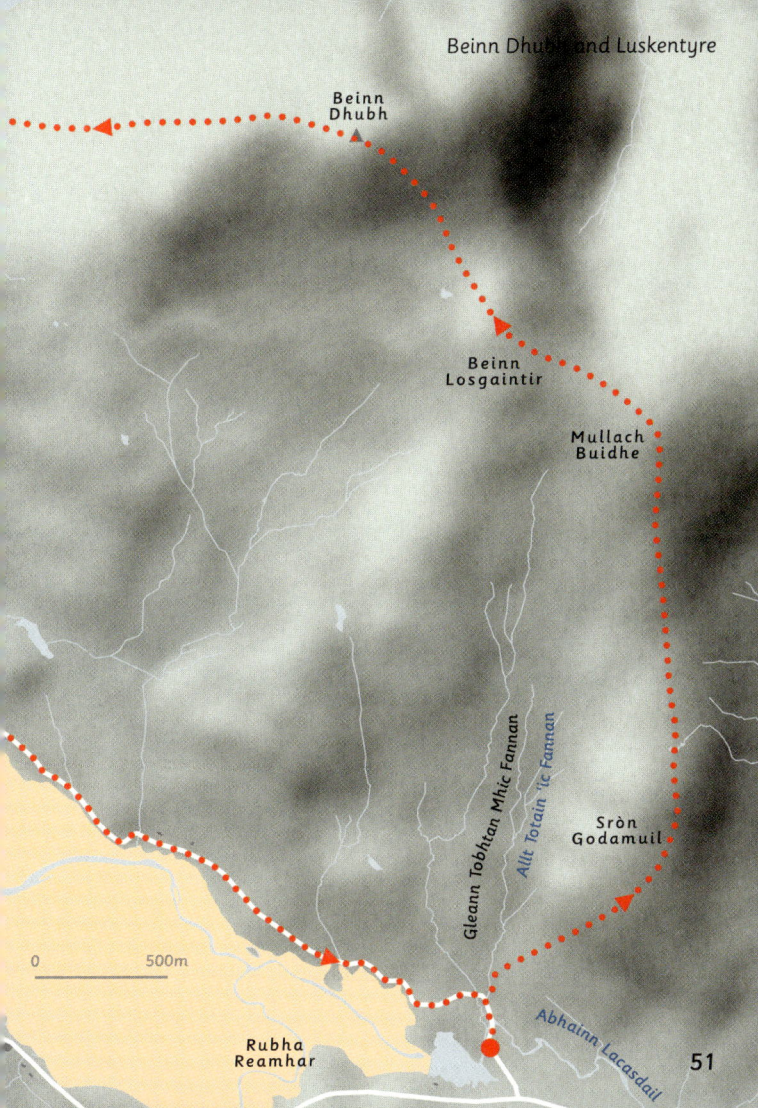

Harris

on the west side of the burn before you reach the shore. Bear southwest and cross rough heather-clad moorland to go through a gate where a fence meets a drystane dyke and then a second gate through the dyke itself.

Walk above Tràigh Rosamol beach, contouring along the grassy and rocky slopes to reach the parking area by the burial ground. From here, you can walk for 4km along the minor road through Luskentyre to the start. Alternatively, continue along the beach, the dunes climbing ever higher as you progress southwestwards before curving southeast with the sands of Tràigh Losgaintir opening out before you. Here, avoid the temptation to cross the outflow of Fadhail Losgaintir and don't stray too far out into the sandflats.

Continue alongside the diminishing dunes to a small burn. Bear left to head north along the edge of the dunes on a trodden path. At the western corner of the burial ground, pass through a gate and follow the path along its edge. After another gate, turn right onto the road to walk back to the start.

Beinn Dhubh and Luskentyre

Beinn Dhubh rising above Tràigh Rosamol

Tràigh Losgaintir

Distance 3.5km **Total ascent** 50m
Time 1 hour 30 **Terrain** sandy beach, dunes, minor road **Map** OS Explorer 455 **Access** nearest bus (W10) from Tarbert and Leverburgh to Luskentyre turning (request stop), 4.5km from the start

Tràigh Losgaintir is much more than just a beach. It's the sparkling white shell sands of Tràigh Rosamol stretching out beneath the conical summit of Beinn Dhubh, backed by huge marram grass-thatched dunes, the sinuous turquoise and silver of the Tràigh Losgaintir tidal sandflats, the huge skies and the views across the sound to the island of Taransay.

Most of all, however, it is the combination of these elements with the views north across Tràigh Rosamol out beyond the coastal waters of Loch a' Siar to the Harris Hills that stops you in your tracks. Not without good reason does its name appear at or near the top of those perennial 'finest beaches' lists.

Remarkably, it is still possible to enjoy a walk along the beaches and dunes at Luskentyre without the company of crowds of other folk doing likewise – despite the increasing number of people visiting the Western Isles in recent years. On a sunny day at the height of summer it can get relatively 'busy', but there are plenty of times year round when you can have the place more or less to yourself. In fact, there's much to recommend Luskentyre for a bracing walk on a wet and windy day, happed up in your waterproofs.

Be aware that sheep and cattle are grazed in the area and there are several ponies as well, so keep dogs close by. It's also worth timing your visit for low tide if at all possible.

Follow the single-track road through Luskentyre to the road end where there is a car park and public toilets. Go through the kissing gate and follow the trodden path alongside the burn to the silver sands of Tràigh Rosamol where you will be left in little doubt as to what all the fuss is about. Turn left and continue along the beach, passing the dunes that climb ever higher as you progress southwestwards.

Across the Sound of Taransay lies the eponymous island, perhaps best known for its starring role in the BBC TV series *Castaway 2000*, which is most often remembered as a 'reality TV' show rather than as the documentary recording the year-long experiment in community building it was intended to be. Divisions in the community and an attendant media circus ultimately detracted from that objective. The best known alumni of the series is the writer and broadcaster, Ben Fogle, a frequent visitor to and advocate for the Isle of Harris. He's well-liked locally.

The beach and dunes curve southwards and then southeast as the sands of Tràigh Losgaintir open out before you, with the settlement of Seilebost at its southern edge and the dunes of Corran Sheileboist pointing northwards across the tidal flats. The sinuous Fadhail Losgaintir winds its way through the sandflats in shifting tones of turquoise through the course of the tides. When the tide is very low, it sometimes seems that you could almost hop across the outflow towards Corran Sheileboist, but avoid the temptation and don't stray too far out into the sandflats.

Continue southeastwards alongside the now diminishing dunes until you reach a small burn. Bear left and head north along the edge of the dunes on a trodden path, soon passing behind the burial ground. At the western corner of the burial ground go through a gate and follow the path along its edge. Go through another gate, turn left on the road (right if you're walking back to catch the bus at the turn-off) and head along the road for 800m to the parking area.

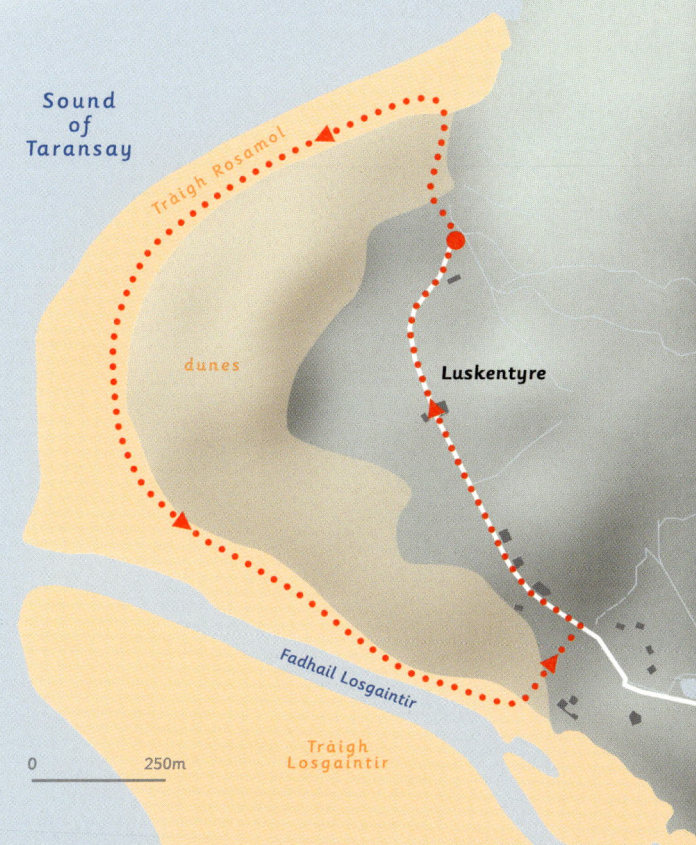

Tràigh Losgaintir

Climbing the steep slope of Sgaoth Iosal

The Skeaudale Horseshoe

Distance 9km **Total ascent** 810m
Time 5 hours **Terrain** rough and rocky hill terrain, potentially boggy ascent to gain the ridge **Map** OS Explorer 456 **Access** bus (W10) to Ceann an Ora from Tarbert and Leverburgh

Rising to the north of the narrow isthmus at Tarbert, between Loch a' Siar and Loch an Tairbeairt, the Skeaudale Horseshoe is the crescent of hills bounding Glen Skeaudale, which descends westwards to the shore of Loch Bun Abhainn Eadarra.

The highest of the horseshoe's five summits, whale-backed Sgaoth Àird (559m) and its angular neighbour Sgaoth Iosal (531m) form the northern rampart of the horseshoe, looming large over the A859 where it crosses the Bealach na Ciste. Across the bealach stands the mighty Clisham and its own horseshoe of attendant summits.

From the A859, Skeaudale's ridges, summits, crags and gullies are mightily impressive yet for reasons mysterious these hills are less frequented than many of their neighbours to the west in the Harris Hills. Perhaps the proximity of the main road is a deterrent, but the sound of traffic is soon left behind and once the first summit – Gillaval Dubh – is reached, an expanse of wild country opens out before you.

The only difficulty on this walk is the steep and strenuous initial climb over rough and often wet ground to gain the ridge. Though 800m of ascent is enough to be getting on with, the climbing is spread out around the horseshoe and feels quite manageable. The irregular, rocky terrain of the southern side of the horseshoe gives way to grassy, gradually-gradiented slopes to the north beyond the Bealach Garbh above the head of Glen Skeaudale. As the terrain changes so does the outlook, with fine views to be enjoyed all the way round.

There is a parking area across the road from the houses just past the Hushinish (Huisinis) turning at Ceann an Ora. From the T-junction, cross the A859 with care. At the end of the crash barrier by the roadsigns, start climbing south over rough ground, zigzagging your way up as necessary. Keep a

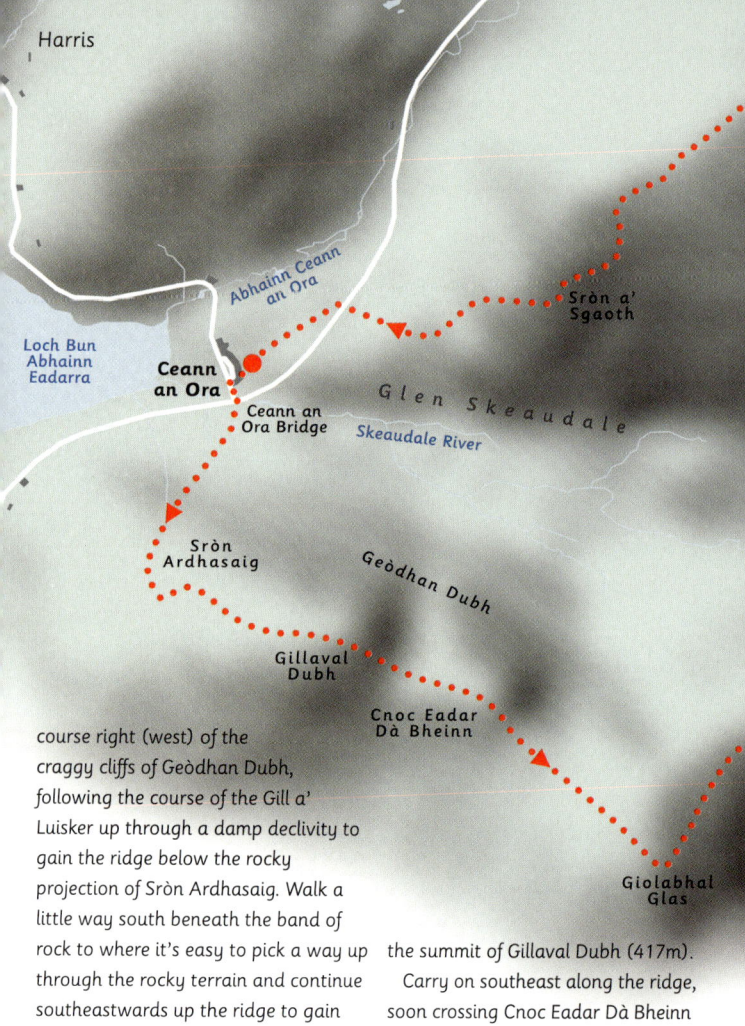

course right (west) of the craggy cliffs of Geòdhan Dubh, following the course of the Gill a' Luisker up through a damp declivity to gain the ridge below the rocky projection of Sròn Ardhasaig. Walk a little way south beneath the band of rock to where it's easy to pick a way up through the rocky terrain and continue southeastwards up the ridge to gain the summit of Gillaval Dubh (417m).

Carry on southeast along the ridge, soon crossing Cnoc Eadar Dà Bheinn

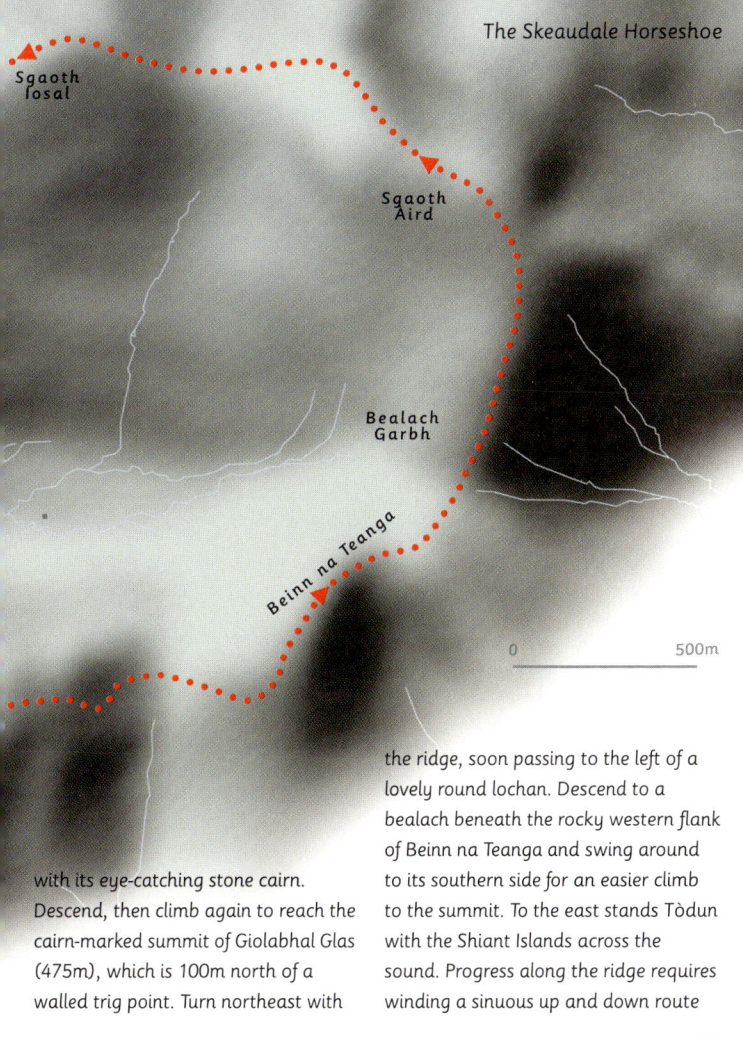

The Skeaudale Horseshoe

with its eye-catching stone cairn.
Descend, then climb again to reach the
cairn-marked summit of Giolabhal Glas
(475m), which is 100m north of a
walled trig point. Turn northeast with
the ridge, soon passing to the left of a
lovely round lochan. Descend to a
bealach beneath the rocky western flank
of Beinn na Teanga and swing around
to its southern side for an easier climb
to the summit. To the east stands Tòdun
with the Shiant Islands across the
sound. Progress along the ridge requires
winding a sinuous up and down route

through the irregular terrain to reach the Bealach Garbh between the heads of Glen Skeaudale and Glen Dibidale dropping away steeply to the east.

There now begins a long but very steady climb up along the broad south ridge of Sgaoth Àird – Gaelic for 'High Wing'. The summit is furnished with a cairn surrounded by a tumbledown shelter wall, which nonetheless does provide some respite on a windy day. The views in all directions are tremendous with Lewis spread out to the north while the hills of South Harris and the Uists stretch away in the opposite direction. Closer to hand, The Clisham and its neighbours dominate the scene. Descend westwards through initially rock-scattered terrain to the bealach east of Sgaoth Iosal.

The ascent of Sgaoth Iosal, 'Low Wing', is easy going up a grassy slope to the narrow summit marked with a couple of small cairns, at the edge of its sheer north face – exercise caution here. You may find scattered about some of the fur and bone pellets regurgitated by the golden eagles who frequent this airy vantage point.

From the summit descend initially southwest along the ridge to Sròn a' Sgaoth. Now descend southwards through the rough, rocky and steep terrain, zigzagging a course as necessary. As you make your way down to the glen, trend westwards as the terrain allows and make for the road around 400m before the turning for Ceann an Ora. On reaching the road cross with care and join the path following the course of the old road down to Ceann an Ora.

Looking east to Beinn na Teanga

The Skeaudale Horseshoe

Harris

Eilean Glas Lighthouse

Scalpay and Eilean Glas

Distance 10km **Total ascent** 200m
Time 3 hours **Terrain** waymarked path, rough and boggy in places; minor road
Map OS Explorer 455 **Access** bus (W14) to Scalpay from Tarbert; get off at Outend (or Scalpay Village if walking the Heritage Path north to south)

Lying at the mouth of Loch an Tairbeairt, the Isle of Scalpay projects into The Minch beyond the easternmost point of Harris.

A bridge connecting the island with Harris was built across the narrow sound in the late 1990s and although this has inevitably brought some change, Scalpay has retained a distinctive character of its own. This derives in part from the sheltered sea lochs, which have made ideal harbours for the island's many creel and fishing boats. The houses crowding around the North Harbour add to the bustling atmosphere of an industrious small fishing port. Indeed, the island's successful shellfish business had been so lucrative in recent times that Hearaich (people from Harris) sometimes referred to Scalpay as 'Treasure Island'.

Despite its modest size – the island is 4km long and 3km wide – Scalpay is home to a population of around 300, but away from the populous west of the island the hinterland feels quite wild. The complete Heritage Trail comprises a loop around Scalpay, either starting near Ceann a Bhàigh at the southern end of the road (also known as Outend); or near another Ceann a' Bhaigh (Bayhead) at the north end of Scalpay, not far from the bridge. A shorter variant loops from Outend around the south coast and back along the Peat Road track (or you can simply retrace your steps).

To accommodate each of these options, the route description for the Heritage Trail is given anti-clockwise, also starting at Ceann a Bhàigh (Outend). For the longer loop, the route follows the path around the south of the island to the magnificent Eilean Glas Lighthouse at the eastern tip, before heading northwest across wild country, eventually reaching the road near the northern Ceann a' Bhaigh (Bayhead).

Harris

The last section of the full loop is a 4km walk along the minor road, which is full of interest and has some great views.

Just before the road runs out at the turning circle at Ceann a Bhàigh, there is a parking area near the start of both the Peat Road track (signed for Eilean Glas Lighthouse) and the coastal footpath to Eilean Glas. Take the latter (signed Coastal Path to Eilean Glas and located a little further down the road), which cuts left up onto a bank above the road. This peaty and sometimes boggy path runs initially southwards through the heather, following the regular marker posts with red and

yellow bands. The path snakes its way up and down through the rough terrain, passing through a gate in a stock fence before dropping into Lag na Làire near the shore. Here, the path bears eastwards and continues on its sinuous way through the undulating terrain before the top of the lighthouse comes into view. Closer to the lighthouse, the path reaches a fine drystane dyke that cuts across the eastern end of the island with Eilean Glas at its tip beyond. Go through a gate in the wall and keep following the marker posts – here the view of the lighthouse and its coterie of outbuildings perched on a rocky outcrop is quite superb. Continue on your way, soon dropping down along a drystane dyke-lined stone path to reach Eilean Glas.

Eilean Glas was the first lighthouse operational in the Outer Hebrides and indeed the first on the west coast of Scotland. It was built between 1787 and 1789 by Thomas Smith, father-in-law of Robert Stevenson, first of the famous Stevenson dynasty of lighthouse builders. Robert Stevenson rebuilt the original tower and Alan Stevenson added the keepers' accommodation in 1824. The 30m tower has two distinctive broad red bands and is everything you could wish an island lighthouse to be.

Once you've thoroughly explored Eilean Glas, return along the stone path, but bear right as you climb rather than returning the way you came. At the top of the rise, keep straight ahead at a three-way signpost signed in two directions for Outend, as well as for Bayhead. This continues northwards to a gate in a section of the drystane dyke that stops abruptly at the edge of a lochan. Go through and follow the gravel track northwards for around 700m to another three-way signpost where the track widens.

To shortcut back to the start, follow this track (now the Peat Track) for 1km to find yourself back at Outend. For the full loop, turn right off the track onto a peaty and often wet path, signed for Bayhead. Follow the marker posts (yellow band near top), which soon begin to climb the flank of Beinn

Sgorabhaig, Scalpay's highest point at a modest 104m. The summit is marked by a cairn and there are great views across Scalpay, Loch an Tairbeairt and north to the empty hills and coastline of the Pàirc area of southeast Lewis with the Shiant Islands lying to its east.

From the summit, the path descends along the northeast ridge of Beinn Sgorabhaig; look out for the marker posts above the south side of Loch Cuilceach. At the western end of the loch, the path crosses a boggy bealach to reach the eastern end of Loch an Dùin where it bears right to climb above its northern side.

Dropping down again, the path goes through a gate in a fence and continues along the north shore of the loch to its western end. Follow the path around to a jetty, crossing a small bridge and going through a gate. Turn right along the track and go right again through a gate by a couple of houses. Bear left and continue to the road.

Unless you have arranged transport from this end of the Heritage Path, continue straight ahead (left) to a T-junction at Ceann a' Bhaigh, turning left to cross a small bridge, then following the road around to the right and through the village. Keep going through a township and at a T-junction turn left and follow the road for a further 3km back to Outend.

Along the way, there are good views across the sea loch to the Bays of Harris and down the island chain on a clear day, while closer to hand are picturesque crofthouses, boats and various maritime gear, and the corrugations of old lazy beds to admire.

Ruins at Gearraidh Lotaigear

Urgha to Rhenigidale on the Postman's Path

Distance 6.5km (one way) or 10km with Moilingeanais detour
Total ascent 475m or 725m with detour **Time** 2 hours 30 or 3 hours 30 with detour **Terrain** metalled track and path for much of the way; single-track road for final stretch to Rhenigidale
Map OS Explorer 456 **Access** bus (W14) to Urgha from Tarbert; bus (W11) to Tarbert from Rhenigidale

The rugged rollercoaster Postman's Path was formerly the only way to reach the remote townships of Moilingeanais, Rhenigidale and Gearraidh Lotaigear from Tarbert – other than by sea.

The construction of the mountain road from Maaruig (Màraig) connected Rhenigidale (Reinigeadal) to the road network in 1989, though the abandoned settlement of Moilingeanais remains just as isolated today as it ever was. Though no longer the lifeline it once was, the route remains popular with walkers, runners and occasional hardy mountain-bikers. It is metalled with stone and gravel for much of the way so consequently the path is well-defined and easy to follow. However, a vague path along the coast between Moilingeanais and the head of Loch Trolamaraig is sketchy and rough going in places. The latter should be avoided for safety reasons, but also because it misses out the descent of the zigzag path known as the Scriob (pronounced *Screeb*, meaning 'slide') with its spectacular airy views. Therefore, backtracking to the main Urgha–Rhenigidale path or leaving Moilingeanais out of your itinerary altogether are the better options.

The walk is enhanced by fine views out to the Shiant Islands and across fjord-like Loch Seaforth, which separates North Harris from the wilds of the Pàirc region of southeast Lewis. The collection of ruined crofthouses at Gearraidh Lotaigear are an eloquent reminder of the fragility of such small remote settlements in times past.

The route can also be walked out and back or extended to make a circular route via Tòdun or the Rhenigidale–Maaruig mountain road.

From the parking area at the southern end of Lochannan Lacasdail, follow the well-defined footpath, signposted for the Gatliff Trust Hostel at Rhenigidale, as it rises steadily eastwards across the moor. As you climb, the elegant ridges of Skeaudale and The Clisham come into view to the northwest. After 2km the path passes a cairn atop the bealach (280m) between Trolamul and Beinn Tharsuinn (NB202009). Descending from the bealach with the Gill Garbh burn to the right, the Shiant Islands can be seen 20km to the east. A narrower path forks across the burn and makes its way down to the abandoned village of Moilingeanais.

For the detour to Moilingeanais, follow the smaller path downhill at the fork, passing through a gate to join a path

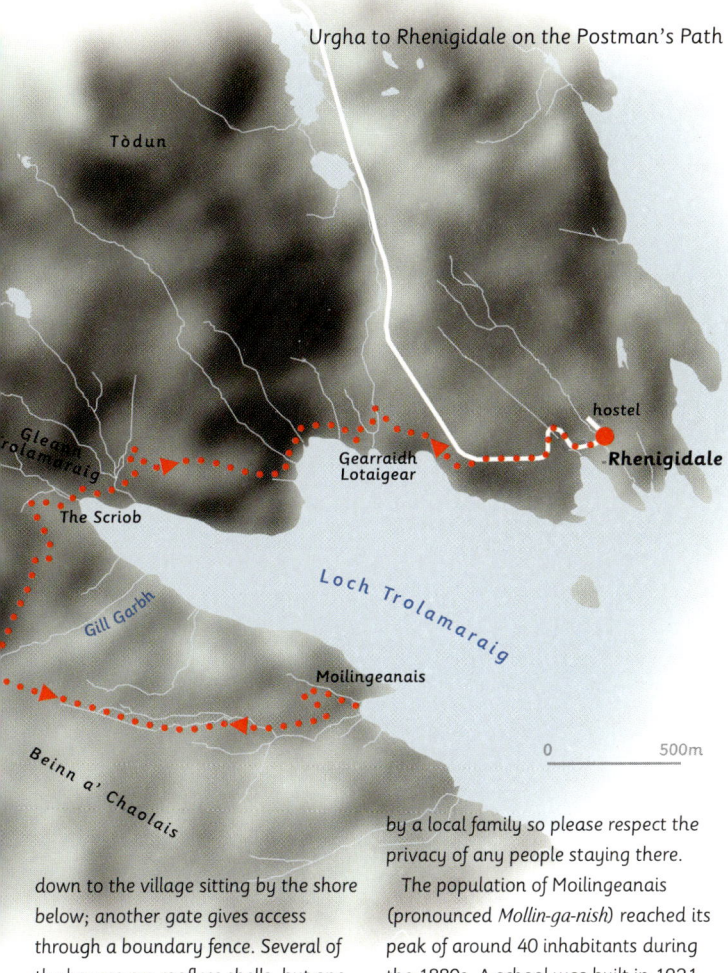

Urgha to Rhenigidale on the Postman's Path

down to the village sitting by the shore below; another gate gives access through a boundary fence. Several of the houses are roofless shells, but one has been renovated for use as a retreat by a local family so please respect the privacy of any people staying there.

The population of Moilingeanais (pronounced *Mollin-ga-nish*) reached its peak of around 40 inhabitants during the 1880s. A school was built in 1921, but in 1935 the authorities withdrew the teacher, effectively closing the school. A lodging allowance was paid for the children to attend school in Tarbert, hence they had to walk five miles (8km) to and from school each week along the Postman's Path, crossing the 280m bealach between Trolamul and Beinn Tharsuinn along the way. The last permanent residents left Moilingeanais in the 1960s.

There is a vague path running above the shore between Moilingeanais and the head of Loch Trolamaraig, and marked on the OS maps, but there are a couple of gully crossings that have become dangerous, so please avoid this route. Retrace your steps from Moilingeanais to rejoin the main path.

If missing out this detour, simply continue along the main path as it descends to a large cairn where you'll have fine views to the sea loch below and out across The Minch. To the north, the boomerang-shaped summit ridge of mighty Tòdun (528m) dominates this corner of North Harris. Beyond the cairn, the path soon begins zigzagging dramatically down the steep flank of Trolamul into Gleann Trolamaraig to reach a footbridge at the head of Loch Trolamaraig.

Cross the bridge and continue over a second footbridge across the Abhainn Kerram. Continue, soon climbing steeply to reach a high point with more great views of the Shiants. Descend again and follow the winding path around the coast, crossing bridges and passing through gates along the way. Shortly before reaching the road, you will pass through the impressive ruins of the old township of Gearraidh Lotaigear.

If you are returning via Maaruig or Tòdun and do not wish to stop off in Rhenigidale, turn left when you reach the road. Otherwise, turn right (east) and continue past a house on your right, soon descending into Rhenigidale. On schooldays the bus for Tarbert can be met in the village at around 4pm. The white-painted Gatliff Trust Hostel sits above the road past the last bend. It's worth a visit or indeed staying for a night or two, although the hostel doesn't take bookings.

The Rhenigidale hostel is one of

three maintained in the Outer Hebrides by the Gatliff Trust, the other two being at Howmore (South Uist) and Berneray. Herbert Gatliff, a retired senior civil servant, established the trust in 1961 to promote the hostelling and outdoor movements. Since then, the Gatliff Trust has continued to maintain its hostels, as well as promoting and supporting understanding of the cultural life and legacy of the people of the Western Isles.

The route can be extended to make a longer circular loop by following the mountain road north and then west towards Maaruig, then taking the path signed for Urgha just before the Abhainn Mhàraig bridge (NB192058). This leads over the Bràigh an Ruisg and through Gleann Lacasdail, with its lochs, to return to Urgha (this makes the total circuit from Urgha 19km with 770m of ascent; allow 6 hours).

Alternatively, it is possible to climb the southeast ridge of Tòdun from the mountain road (NB221022). From the summit, descend the north ridge to the 200m contour, then head west to cross the Abhainn Loch an Reithe before cutting across the plateau beneath the northern flank of Stràthabhal and descending northwest to the Bràigh an Ruisg. Follow the path down through Gleann Lacasdail to return to Urgha. This route is tough going in places and requires navigational competence.

Harris

On the Postman's Path with the Shiant Islands (centre) on the horizon

Urgha to Rhenigidale on the Postman's Path

Harris

Tòdun seen from the southeast

Stràthabhal, An Reithe and Tòdun

Distance 10.75km **Total ascent** 675m
Time 4 hours 30 **Terrain** rough, rocky hill and moorland terrain; boggy in places **Map** OS Explorer 456
Access bus (W11) to the Abhainn Mhàraig bridge (request stop) from Tarbert

The distinctive fin of Tòdun's summit ridge stands in majestic isolation, presiding over the far northeast corner of Harris. It also seems to snag any passing weather so that rainclouds appear to rotate around it on a slow-motion spin cycle. However, when visibility is good, the views from Tòdun's summit can be tremendous – especially out across The Minch to Skye and the mainland's western seaboard.

Tòdun is usually climbed from the mountain road to the north and this is certainly the easiest and quickest route of ascent and descent. This longer circular route taking in the minor summits of neighbouring Stràthabhal and An Reithe makes for a more satisfying walk as it explores Tòdun's wild hinterland.

There are good opportunities for spotting red deer, mountain hares – especially when in their winter coats – and golden eagles. The latter can be seen perched on a prominent rock on Tòdun's southeast ridge a short distance beyond the summit; the ground around is often strewn with regurgitated fur and bone pellets. If you're lucky you may get a close-quarters fly-past.

Park carefully next to the road by the Abhainn Mhàraig bridge, then head south away from the Maaruig (Màraig) road junction and go through a gate on your right where the road bends. Follow the path gently uphill to intersect with the main Maaruig–Urgha path. Turn left (south) to continue gently climbing. The Clisham climbs above the A859 to the northwest while the angular ridges of Sgaoth Àird dominate the skyline to the southwest. After 600m, with Loch an

Stràthabhal, An Reithe and Tòdun

Ruisg on your right, bear left off the path and strike out southeast up the often wet, peaty, tussocky slope. It's a bit of a slog to start with but the going gets easier as the ground becomes rockier higher up.

Eventually you'll gain a rocky high point at 257m. Contour around the rocky outcrops to a wet, peaty plateau and bear obliquely southeast across this to pick up the north ridge of Stràthabhal, dodging peat hags as best you can. Once on the ridge all becomes straightforward and the summit, marked with a stone cairn, is reached at 389m. There are fine views across southeast Harris and over to Skye. Lose a little height dropping to a bealach that holds a small lochan, skirting to the left of the lower summit (380m) with views southeast to lovely Loch an Reithe nestled in the corrie below and An Reithe and Tòdun rising beyond. Descend steadily towards the southern end of Loch an Reithe and cross the outflow where easiest below the loch.

Looking up at the southwest flank of An Reithe, you will see an obvious heathery rake climbing obliquely up the flank. Follow this up for 100m to gain the summit at 430m. Descend the eastern flank of An Reithe, picking a route between boulders and loose rock. Aim for the high point of the bealach, crossing next to a small lochan to gain Tòdun's western flank. Climb initially northwards, tackling the steep hillside obliquely, before bearing southeast towards the summit ridge as the gradient eases a little.

The summit (528m) is marked with an OS trig point surrounded by a low shelter wall. The views are impressive. To the northwest, The Clisham and its coterie of Harris Hills dominate the skyline; to the east across Loch Seaforth lies the wild fastness of Pàirc with stunning views across The Minch to the mountainous western seaboard of mainland Scotland. It's worth descending along the narrowing southeast ridge a little for the view over Rhenigidale and Loch Trolamaraig.

From the summit, head back northwards along the ridge, looking out for useful stretches of trodden path as you begin descending. Follow the ridge down as far as possible, bearing northeast (right) to cross the burn and join the road just above the series of sharp bends to avoid too much boggy ground. Follow the road down to and then alongside Loch Màraig for 2km to return to the Abhainn Mhàraig bridge.

Tòdun direct route

Park carefully in one of the small off-road parking areas (or ask to be let down by the bus) in the vicinity of the northernmost of the lochans along the mountain road. Leave the road by the outflow of the lochan, skirt along its edge, then strike out southwest over rough often boggy ground. At the foot of the steeper ground, bear initially northwest to climb up towards the lower slopes of Tòdun's north ridge. Swing around to the north, as the terrain allows, to gain the north ridge. Continue following the ridgeline, using the traces of trodden path as they appear. The gradient steepens as you climb and the path weaves through some rocky ground as you approach the summit.

The summit (528m) is marked with an OS trig point surrounded by a low shelter wall. Retrace your outward route on the descent.

Looking across The Minch from near the summit of Tòdun

Stràthabhal, An Reithe and Tòdun

Todun rising above Rhenigidale from Ard Caol

Rhenigidale and Loch Seaforth

Distance 2.5km **Total ascent** 105m
Time 1 hour 30 **Terrain** rugged coastal headlands, rough path, boggy in places; some exposed areas requiring care
Map OS Explorer 456 **Access** bus (W11) (twice daily) to Rhenigidale from Tarbert

The small clachan of Rhenigidale (Reinigeadal) has a claim to fame in that it was the last settlement in the UK to be connected to the road network in 1989.

The 6km extension from the neighbouring village of Maaruig (Màraig) came after years of campaigning by the indefatigable Kenny Mackay who, among other incarnations, was for some years the village postman, delivering the mail (as well as groceries and medicines) thrice-weekly along the rugged rollercoaster Postman's Path from Urgha.

Rhenigidale is a crofting settlement and is home to one of the Gatliff Trust's three Hebridean hostels; it has a small pebble beach and an old quay where supplies were formerly delivered by sea from Scalpay. In the summer months many visitors drive along the winding mountain road to Rhenigidale, maybe take a couple of snaps and off they drive again. They are, however, missing a trick. A short walk just to the north of Rhenigidale brings you to the headlands overlooking the mouth of fjord-like Loch Seaforth and the wild hinterland of Pàirc beyond.

There is a good chance you'll see some wildlife when wandering around the points: seals, porpoises, dolphins, otters, gannets, ravens, golden and white-tailed eagles, among other species, all frequent the area.

The route described here can be walked in either direction and there is also scope for further exploration should you wish. Remember, though, that sheep are grazed here so please close all gates behind you (unless they are tied open) and keep dogs on a lead.

Park carefully and considerately in the village (the passing places by the postbox and opposite the hostel are used for parking). To the left of the house called Sith-Phort at the last bend in the road, go through a gate and head

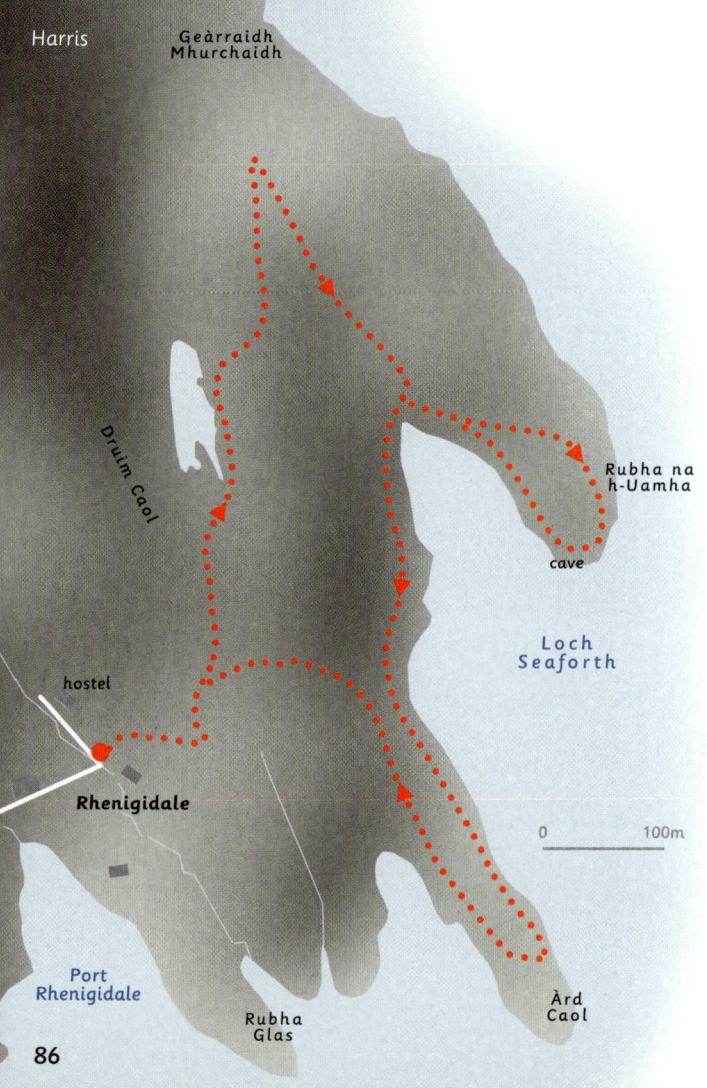

up the often boggy slope to go through another gate on your right. Follow the vague zigzag to the top of the brae. Here you'll find the first of a series of marker posts with yellow discs near their tops. Head crosscountry, following these posts, with some fine views opening up to the east across The Minch.

Go through a gate with a sign reading Geàrraidh Mhurchaidh and continue following marker posts past a little spring-fed lochan to a bealach marked with a small cairn of stones. There are views along Loch Seaforth and directly north across the water to the Pàirc region of southeast Lewis with the craggy eminence of Caiteseal (pronounced *Kate-uh-shall*) rising 440m straight out of the loch.

Walk down the rocky path with care to arrive at the final marker post in the glen below. Respect the privacy of the people living in the house just to the north and turn southeast, descending gently along the glen back to the coast. Here, you can make a detour around the headland of Rubha na h-Uamha (Point of the Cave) by bearing left around the head of the inlet. Otherwise continue right, following the faint path around the south side of the inlet. A small-scale version of the Isle of Skye's Bad Step presents an obstacle which can be avoided by simply dropping below it to continue on your way. The rough path brings you to a metal gate on the other side of which is Àrd Caol.

Continue around this splendid headland with its views across Loch Seaforth and The Minch: the Shiants, Torridon and the Cuillin are all in view on a clear day. Follow the indistinct trodden path back up along the spine of Àrd Caol, bearing left through a damp declivity to arrive in sight of the telegraph poles and marker posts that will lead you back down to Rhenigidale and its noteworthy road.

Harris

Looking northeast across to Àrd Caol with Pàirc beyond

Harris

The Clisham Horseshoe

Distance 13.5km **Total ascent** 1065m **Time** 7 hours **Terrain** rough and rocky ridges, potentially very boggy approach and return; some bouldery sections and one exposed descent requiring caution **Map** OS Explorer 456 **Access** bus (W10) to the bridge over the Abhainn Sgaladail (NB183099) before Ardvourlie (request stop) from Tarbert

The Clisham (An Cliseam) is generally climbed from the southeast, from a parking place along the A859. This makes for a short sharp climb of 650m over 3km that can be recommended only for the views or for those with limited time.

By contrast, the Clisham Horseshoe is a fine day's walk. Approaching The Clisham from the northeast, a long walk in on an often boggy path brings you to the foot of the ridge connecting Mullach an Langa, Mulla bho Thuath, Mulla bho Dheas and The Clisham itself. There is some easy scrambling on the ridge and

The Clisham from the bealach on its western side

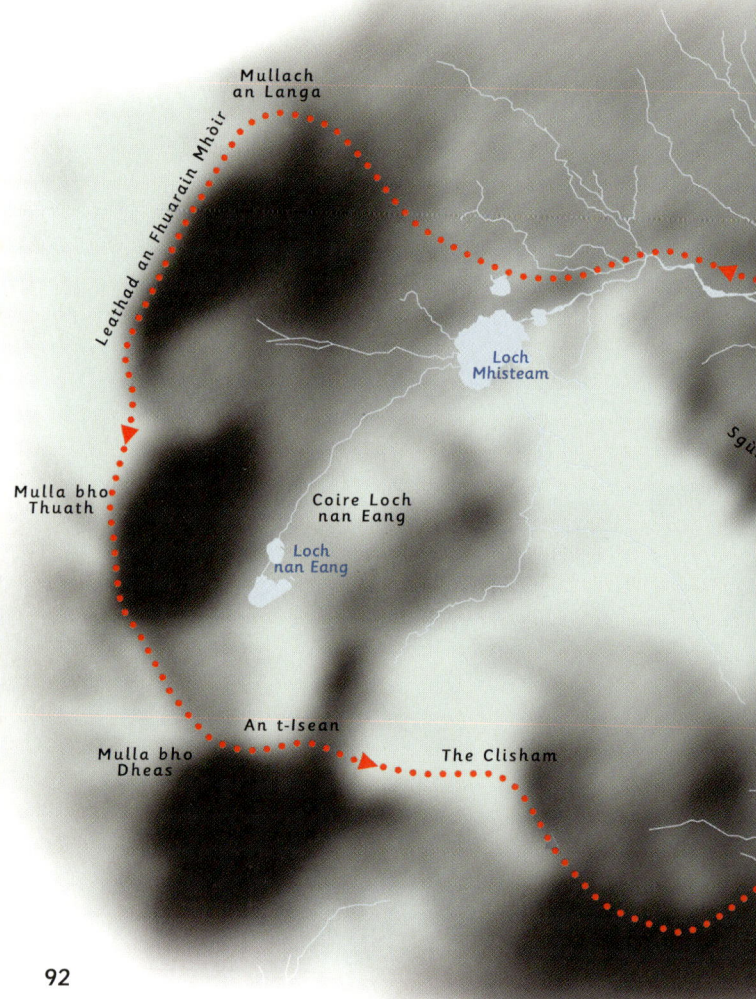

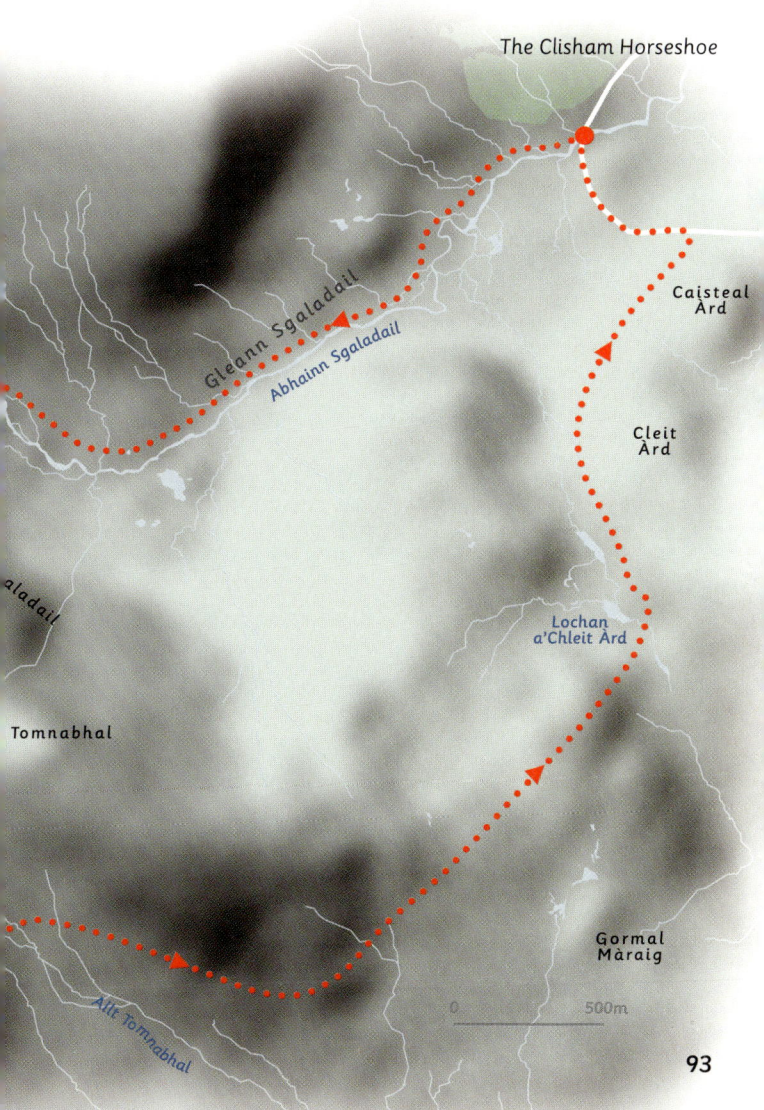

tougher sections that are easily avoided. This is an enjoyable route for those who are confident on rocky terrain with some exposure, but it's not a walk for beginners – especially in poor visibility. On a clear day, a traverse of the ridge with The Clisham ahead of you is a real Hebridean classic.

There is limited parking by the bridge over the Abhainn Sgaladail, which is 800m south of the Scaladale Centre at Ardvourlie, or 500m up the road towards Tarbert on the roadside verge at the start of the Hebridean Way and Harris Walkway (NB187096). From the bridge, pick up the often very boggy path (marked on the OS Explorer) heading up Gleann Sgaladail along the north side of the Abhainn Sgaladail. The path is fairly distinct for much of the way up to Loch Mhisteam where it disappears definitively, leaving you to pick a route across rough ground to gain the east ridge of Mullach an Langa (NB143094).

The ascent starts easily enough but soon steepens over rough vegetation, though the ground becomes drier underfoot. This is the hardest section of the entire horseshoe, but as you gain height the view north to Loch Langabhat opens up to reward your efforts. The gradient eventually relents before a final steep pull up through a boulderfield. From the summit (614m), marked by a small cairn, you can survey the route ahead, around the horseshoe to The Clisham.

Continue south along the ridge with no difficulties – a rocky section between two crags is easier going than it looks – to gain the grassy ridge leading to the summit of Mulla bho Thuath (720m). The view ahead onto Mulla bho Dheas is magnificent and in clear conditions the sparkling white beaches of South Harris can be seen to the southwest. Descend southwards along a path to the bealach, crossing a distinctive quartz band, then follow the ridge as it turns southeast to reach the cairned summit of Mulla bho Dheas (743m).

The descent eastwards along the ridge from here involves some fairly tricky scrambling. This can be avoided by following a path leaving the summit *immediately west of the cairn, heading east, dropping down and then traversing along the northern side of the ridge – care is required as the path is exposed and slippery. The path regains the ridge at the bealach to the west of the subsidiary top of An t-Isean. A path ascends An t-Isean, bypassing some crags, then a long grassy descent delivers you to the foot of The Clisham. The climb is steep, initially grassy then rocky, although the bouldery ground can be avoided until just below the summit. A small cairn marks the northern end of the summit ridge – there are sublime views back along the horseshoe. Continue to the summit (799m), where a trig point is enclosed by a large shelter wall.*

Once you've soaked up the views (and hopefully not the weather) from the highest point in the Outer Hebrides, head southeast down the ridge, following the clear path worn by those climbing The Clisham directly from the A859. Higher up, the path is dry as it winds its way through rocky terrain, but the going becomes wetter further down. Continue down the ridge until you reach easier ground, turning left here to traverse north, then east around the headwaters of the Allt Tomnabhal.

Skirt beneath the prominent rock slabs on the southeastern flank of Tomnabhal, keeping to the easier ground before swinging northeast across rough terrain, making for three small lochans (NB184083) lying directly west of Cleit Àrd. From the lochans, continue northwards along the green track of the Hebridean Way (also the Harris Walkway), which is boggy in places, to reach the main road after 1.5km.

Harris

Heading along the Abhainn Sgaladail

Harris

Looking west across Loch Chleistir

The Glens of North Harris

Distance 17km **Total ascent** 560m
Time 6 hours **Terrain** metalled tracks and good paths, with some boggy sections **Map** OS Explorer 456
Access outward bus (W10) to the Bowglass parking area 1.5km north of Ardvourlie at the mouth of Gleann Bhiogadail (request stop) from Tarbert and Stornoway; return bus (W12) to Hushinish (Huisinis) and Tarbert from Meavaig (Miabhaig)

The wild hinterland of the North Harris Hills is the setting for a tour of three glens – Bhiogadail, Langadail and Mhiabhaig. This route passes a number of freshwater lochs, including the 13km-long Loch Langabhat, taking in some fine mountain scenery with good opportunities for spotting golden eagles en route.

The route covers a fair distance, but progress is aided by good paths and tracks throughout. As this is a linear walk you'll need to arrange transport at either end. Alternatively it can be walked as an out and return route from either end to Loch Chleistir, sitting beneath the northwest ridge of Stulabhal, which is roughly the midway point.

From the parking area at the mouth of Gleann Bhiogadail, go through the kissing gate next to a stock gate and begin the steady climb westwards along a good track. Walkers with dogs should be aware that there are often cattle – including Highland cows – grazing loose in this area. After 3km the path crosses the Bealach na h-Uamha where the view opens up westwards to Stulabhal and northwards to the improbably immense landlocked Loch Langabhat stretching away into Lewis beyond.

Follow the rough track down into Gleann Langadail, keeping right where the path forks. Cross the Abhainn Langadail on the sturdy bridge and begin the long steady climb up the western flank of the glen (300m over the course of 2km) in a series of deep zigzags.

Cross the Braigh an Iachlachain at 328m and descend steadily beneath the craggy north face of Stulabhal with

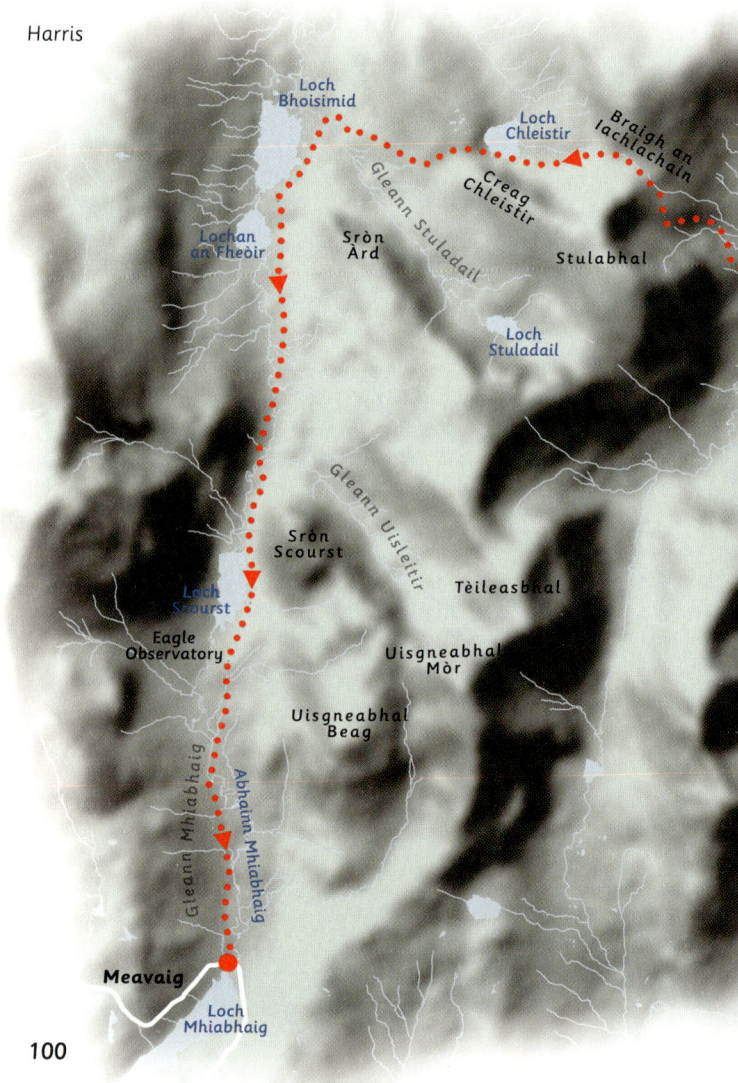

The Glens of North Harris

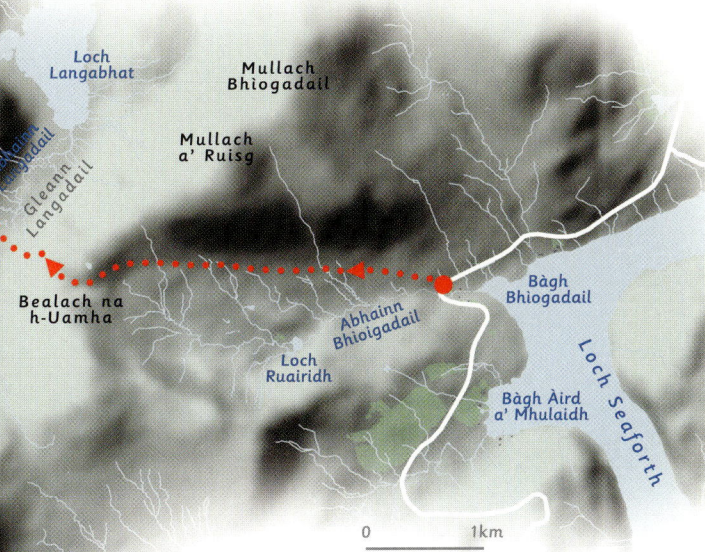

picturesque Loch Chleistir sitting plumb in the corrie below. To the north lies the remote region of Ceann Loch Reasort with the wilds of southwest Lewis beyond. Continue past Loch Chleistir, cross a bealach and descend steadily on a good path cutting diagonally down into the glen below. Follow the path round towards Loch Bhoisimid, cross a bridge and join a broader metalled track by a substantial timber-clad bothy used by stalking and fishing parties.

Walk south along the glen track, passing the impressive prow of Sròn Scourst after about 3km. Sitting next to the track overlooking Loch Scourst, you will find the North Harris Eagle Observatory, built and maintained by the North Harris Trust. Unsurprisingly, this is a great spot for observing eagles, but it's also a great place to shelter and contemplate the view, eagles or no.

Continue down the glen track for a further 3km, crossing the bridge over the Abhainn Mhiabhaig before reaching the road and parking area at Meavaig.

The Glens of North Harris

Looking north along Loch Langabhat

Harris

Teileasbhal (right) and Uisgneabhal Mòr seen from the east

Stulabhal, Tèileasbhal and Uisgneabhal Mòr

Distance 20km (shorter route 12.5km) **Total ascent** 1200m (shorter route 930m) **Time** 8 hours (shorter route 5 hours) **Terrain** good track and path to start, followed by pathless and occasionally rough and boggy mountain and moorland terrain **Map** OS Explorer 456 **Access** bus (W12) to Meavaig (Miabhaig) from Hushinish (Huisinis) and Tarbert

Of the hills on the eastern side of Gleann Mhiabhaig, the distinctive summit of Stulabhal is something of an outlier. This long day's route brings that hill into the fold with those rising to the west of Gleann Eadarra – Tèileasbhal and Uisgneabhal Mòr, second highest summit of the Outer Hebrides.

This is a spectacular and quite demanding day's hillwalking, taking in three summits in excess of 600m; therefore, a shorter option omitting Stulabhal is incorporated in the route description here. A good level of navigational competence is required to negotiate the convoluted and often pathless hill terrain once the tracks are left behind. The long initial walk in along Gleann Mhiabhaig is full of grand scenery and passes the North Harris Trust's Eagle Observatory, which tells you what you need to know about the chances of spotting certain large raptors in the vicinity.

From the parking area at the head of Loch Mhiabhaig, follow the Landrover track north up Gleann Mhiabhaig, soon crossing a bridge over the Abhainn Mhiabhaig, with the monolithic buttress of Sròn Scourst dominating the view ahead. Pass by the splendidly-situated eagle observatory, which sits above the track overlooking the outflow of Loch Scourst. Pass the loch and an estate bothy shortly after. Continuing up the track, the northern aspect of Sròn Scourst looks even more impressive.

For the main route, carry on beneath the narrowing ridge of Sròn Ard, which descends towards the end of the main

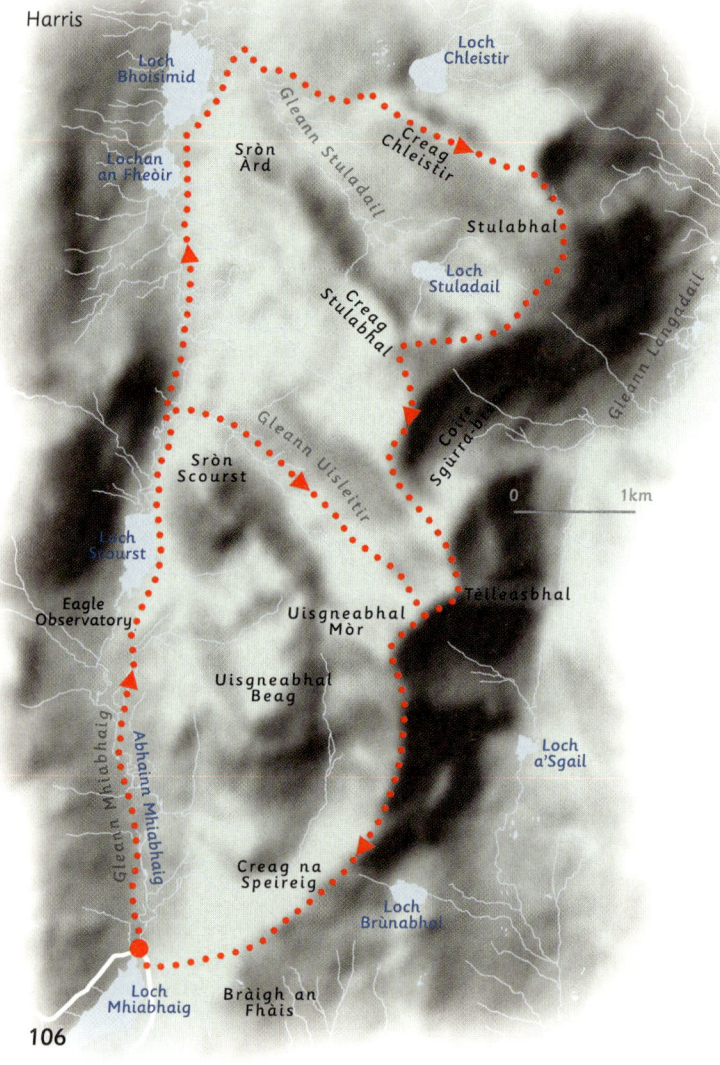

Stulabhal, Tèileasbhal and Uisgneabhal Mòr

track just short of Loch Bhoisimid. There is a smart timber-clad bothy used by fishing and stalking parties here. Bear right onto a smaller path that winds away northeast before crossing the Stuladail River via a sturdy footbridge, now turning southeast directly to climb towards the northwest ridge of Stulabhal. Leave the path where it starts to bear northeast towards Loch Chleistir. Begin the initially steep, rough ascent of Creag Chleistir, zigzagging through rocky terrain to gain easier ground higher up. Continue along the ridge to the summit of Stulabhal (579m), marked with a trig point enclosed by a stone shelter wall. The distinctive twin summits of Uisgneabhal Mòr and Tèileasbhal rise to the southwest while northwestwards beyond the Harris Hills the Uig Hills of southwest Lewis can be seen.

Head initially southeast along the ridge before bearing southwest to descend (with care) the steep and often wet south flank for over 200m to the bealach below. To the west of the bealach Loch Stuladail sits nestled in the corrie beneath the cliffs of Creag Stulabhal. Continue up the eastern ridge of Creag Stulabhal to reach its summit (513m), then bear south around the head of Coire Sgùrra-breac and climb the rock-strewn slopes steadily to the summit of Tèileasbhal (697m) with a little easy scrambling over large rocky blocks to reach the summit cairn.

If you're leaving Stulabhal out of your itinerary then once you've crossed the footbridge over the Abhainn Uisleitir, bear right and begin climbing on initially steep, rough and wet ground, keeping the burn on your right. Cross a tributary and continue on up into Gleann Uisleitir, bearing southeast. Climb to drier ground on the eastern flank of the glen, looking out for old trodden paths to aid progress. As you continue climbing through the glen, aim for the left-hand side of the bealach ahead, which lies between Tèileasbhal (left) and Uisgneabhal Mòr.

Approaching the bealach there is some rocky ground to cross, but no real difficulty is involved. From the bealach bear left (northeast) and climb the ridge to the summit of Tèileasbhal.

The summit of Uisgneabhal Mòr lies less than 1km away as the crow flies (and back the way you've just come if you've missed out Stulabhal). The sharp descent of 140m down to the bealach is followed by a 180m climb over initially very steep bouldery ground before easing a little and giving way to grassy slopes higher up. The cairn-marked summit is atop a prominent crag overlooking the bealach; pass to its right, then cut back to reach the cairn (729m). There are fine views along the beach-infested coast of South Harris to soak up before you move on again.

Carry on along the crag-edged ridge before bearing south across open ground to begin descending the south ridge. Initially the going is easy along the grassy well-defined ridge, but the ground becomes increasingly rough and boggy lower down. Cross the summit of Creag na Speireig and keep to high ground as much as possible to cross Braigh an Fhais (217m). Descend a short way to a small lochan on the ridge and from here descend the steep, wet, rough ground westwards to reach the B887 a little way short of the Gleann Mhiabhaig parking area.

Heading up Gleann Uisleitir with the prow of Sròn Scourst behind

Stulabhal, Tèileasbhal and Uisgneabhal Mòr

Climbing to the summit of Cleiseabhal with Oireabhal beyond

Muladal, Ulabhal, Oireabhal and Cleiseabhal

Distance 16km **Total ascent** 980m
Time 6 hours **Terrain** good track and path to start, followed by pathless, rough, occasionally boggy mountain and moorland terrain; short road section to end **Map** OS Explorer 456 **Access** bus (W12) to Gleann Chliostair turning (request stop) from Tarbert and Hushinish (Huisinis)

A traverse of the elegant ridge of Harris Hills forming the boundary between Gleann Mhiabhaig to the east and Gleann Chliostair to the west makes for a manageable and spectacular hillwalking day out.

The northern end of the ridge is gained after a long walk in through Gleann Chliostair on the track servicing the hydropower station and reservoir and the stalkers' path that ultimately leads down to Loch Uladail beneath the magnificent buttress of Sròn Uladail. A steady 200m climb from the path delivers you to the summit of Muladal – the jumping-off point for 6.5km of rollercoaster ridge-walking splendour, taking in the summits of Ulabhal, Oireabhal, Cleiseabhal and the rocky knoll of Bidigidh along the way. Fine views abound with the surrounding Harris Hills, the beaches, bays and hills of southwest Harris and the island of Taransay all catching the eye as you progress. This is also prime golden eagle-spotting country, so remember to scan the skies now and then.

Before reaching Amhuinnsuidhe Castle on the B887 from Tarbert towards Hushinish, turn right along a minor road and follow it for 500m to the turning for a fish farm. Park carefully here. If using the bus, ask to be let down by the Gleann Chliostair turning.

Pass around the gate across the track heading north, continue along the glen, passing Loch Leòsaid, then cross the bridge over the Abhainn Leòsaid. Carry on along the track road, past the hydropower station, then climb steadily up through the glen. The path swings right, passing beneath the pipeline from

Loch Chliostair before climbing in a wide bend to reach the dam at the outflow of Loch Chliostair.

The path continues along the eastern side of Loch Chliostair beneath the flanks of Oireabhal and Ulabhal, with fine views of Tiorga Mòr's eastern aspect across the loch. Near the head of the loch, cross a bridge and climb a little to reach Loch Aiseabhat. Cross the outflow of the loch on stepping stones and follow the path along its western edge. Beyond the head of the loch, before the stalkers' path drops away on its descent to Loch Uladail, leave the path and climb initially east, then northeastwards for 200m on reasonably wet and rough ground to the gently rounded summit of Muladal (454m), a fine vantage point for surveying the empty hinterland of Loch Reàsort.

Bear south and drop a little to cross the bealach before beginning the climb south along the steep north ridge of Ulabhal, soon picking your way through and across the broken rock bands higher up to reach the cairn-marked summit at 659m. The summit of Ulabhal provides one of the finest vantage points in all of Harris – on a clear day the views take in a panorama of mountains, lochs, coastline and sea. Continue south down the long narrowing ridge, skirting to the right of a rocky outcrop before arriving at a bealach (564m) with views eastwards into the impressive Cathadail an Ear, which drops dramatically down into Gleann Mhiabhaig. From the bealach, tackle the low crag in front of you straight on, then begin the easy climb southwest to the summit of Oireabhal at 662m.

From the summit of Oireabhal, descend steeply along the southern ridge to a bealach at 460m, then climb a short way up and over the rocky knoll of Bìdigidh (500m). Descend south to another bealach at 425m, then begin the final climb along the ridge which swings to the west before reaching the trig point at the summit of Cleiseabhal (512m). Despite its relatively modest height, Cleiseabhal has a sweeping outlook southwest onto Taransay and along the coast of South Harris to North Uist beyond.

Muladal, Ulabhal, Oireabhal and Cleiseabhal

Avoid the steeper ground to the west as you leave the summit by descending the long southwest ridge as if aiming for the island of Sòdhaigh Mòr. Once you reach Mulla Chleiseabhal, swing westwards to meet the B887 near Loch nan Caor. Turn right along the road and follow it for 1.5km back to the start.

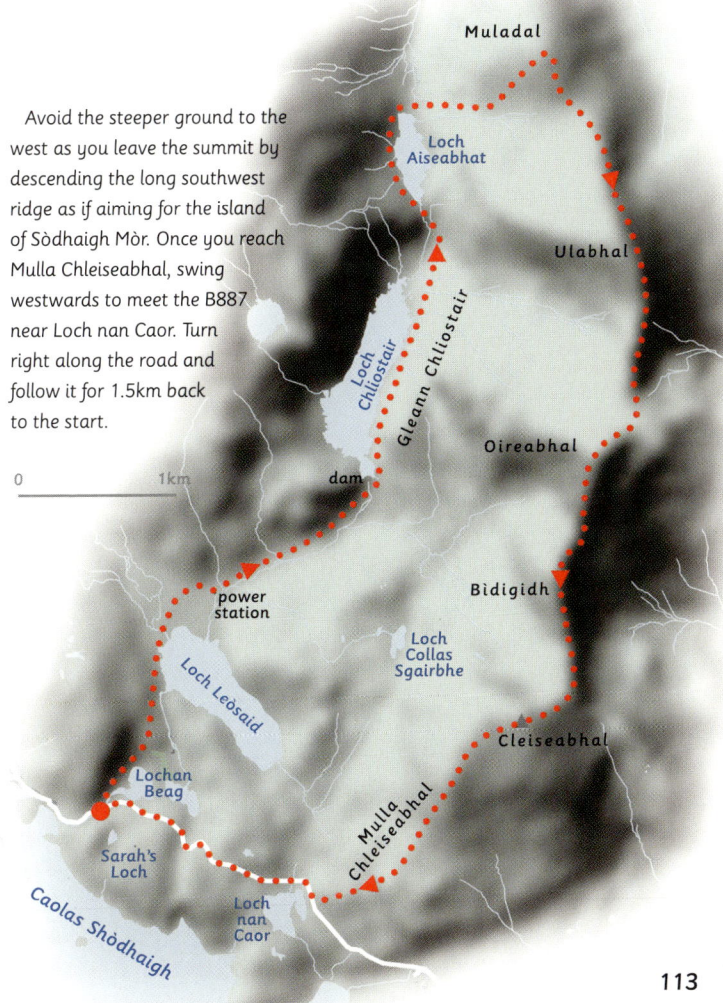

Harris

Sròn Uladail and Loch Uladail seen from Tiorga Beag

Loch Chliostair and Gleann Uladail

Distance 14.5km **Total ascent** 505m
Time 4 hours 30 **Terrain** track roads, metalled tracks and good paths, some boggy sections on the path between Loch Aiseabhat and Loch Uladail
Map OS Explorer 456 **Access** bus (W12) to Gleann Chliostair turning (request stop) from Tarbert and Hushinish (Huisinis)

The overhanging buttress of Sròn Uladail stands a long way from the nearest road. Rather handily, however, a power station track and a stalkers' path lead through some fine mountain country to deliver walkers right to the doorstep of this impressive truncated spur, with its distinctive profile and daunting 370m cliffs carved by ice flowing down Gleann Uladail.

Although this route benefits from easy to follow tracks and paths, they lead you deep into wild mountainous terrain, so you will need to be appropriately prepared and equipped.

This is golden eagle country so keep your eyes on the skies when not watching your step. There's also a good likelihood of seeing some red deer in Gleann Uladail particularly.

Before reaching Amhuinnsuidhe Castle on the B887 from Tarbert towards Hushinish, turn right along a minor road and follow it for 500m to the turning for a fish farm. Park carefully here. If using the bus, ask to be let down by the Gleann Chliostair turning.

Pass around the gate across the track heading north, continuing along the glen past Loch Leòsaid and over the bridge across the Abhainn Leòsaid. Carry on along the track road, passing the hydropower station, then climbing steadily up the glen. The path swings right beneath the pipeline from Loch Chliostair before climbing in a wide bend to reach the dam at the outflow of Loch Chliostair.

The path skirts along the eastern edge of Loch Chliostair, hemmed in on that side by the flanks of Oireabhal and Ulabhal, but with fine views of Tiorga Mòr's eastern aspect across the loch. Near the head of the loch, cross a bridge and climb a little to reach Loch Aiseabhat. Cross the outflow of the loch on stepping stones and follow the path along its western edge. Beyond the head of the loch, the path begins its 2km descent down through Gleann Uladail, beneath the flanks of Muladal and Sròn Uladail.

Several burns run off the hills, making the ground boggy in places. The path eventually runs out by a fishing hut on the shore of Loch Uladail, beneath the magnificent overhanging buttress of Sròn Uladail. In 2010 a live BBC broadcast, *The Great Climb*, followed the progress of two climbers, Dave MacLeod and Tim Emmett, battling to scale the 370m cliff. Retrace your outward route to Amhuinnsuidhe Castle.

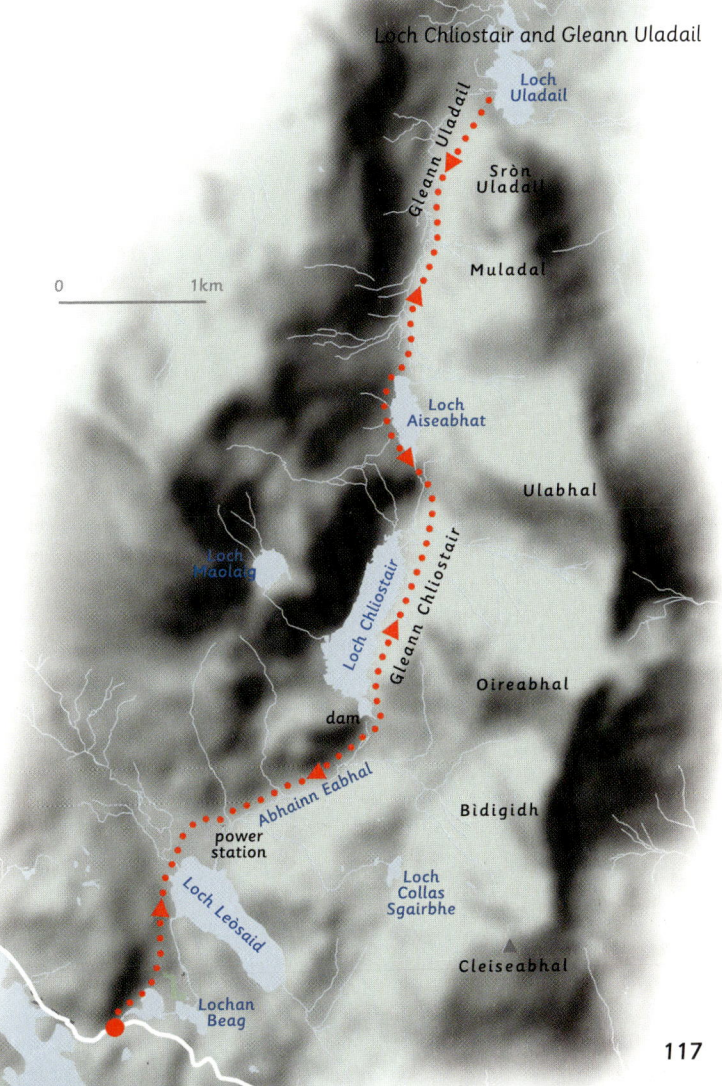

Loch Chliostair and Gleann Uladail

Sròn Uladail and Loch Uladail seen from the northwest

Descending towards Tiorga Beag from Tiorga Mòr

Harris Hills and Loch Rèasort backpack

Distance 32km **Total ascent** 2050m
Time 2 days **Terrain** mountain and moorland; often pathless, very rough and boggy in places **Map** OS Explorer 456 **Access** bus (W12) to Gleann Chliostair turning (request stop) from Tarbert and Hushinish (Huisinis)

This route makes the most of the rugged country of the western Harris Hills. The outward leg heads north over Tiorga Mòr, along the ridge flanking Gleann Uladail and ultimately to the wilderness at the head of Loch Rèasort. The return leg heads south along the ridge on the eastern side of the glen, taking in the summits of Ulabhal, Oireabhal and Cleiseabhal.

Day 1

Distance 16km **Total ascent** 1000m
Time 9 hours

Before reaching Amhuinnsuidhe Castle on the B887 from Tarbert towards Hushinish, turn right along a minor road and follow it for 500m to the turning for a fish farm. Park carefully here. If using the bus, ask to be let down by the Gleann Chliostair turning.

Pass around the gate across the track heading north, continuing along the glen past Loch Leòsaid and over the bridge across the Abhainn Leòsaid. Carry on along the track road, passing the hydropower station, then climbing steadily up the glen. Just before the track heads beneath the pipeline from Loch Chliostair, turn left off the track, climbing northwest on rough ground before gaining a level area just above the loch. Now climb steeply up the southeast ridge of Tiorga Mòr, passing above Loch Maolaig, nestled in its corrie. This steepest section of the ridge is rocky and rough, but grassy gullies aid progress. The gradient eases as the rocky ground is cleared and a vague path leads towards the rock-crested summit of Tiorga Mòr, with its trig point and drystane shelter wall. There are fine views all around: east, beyond the

Harris

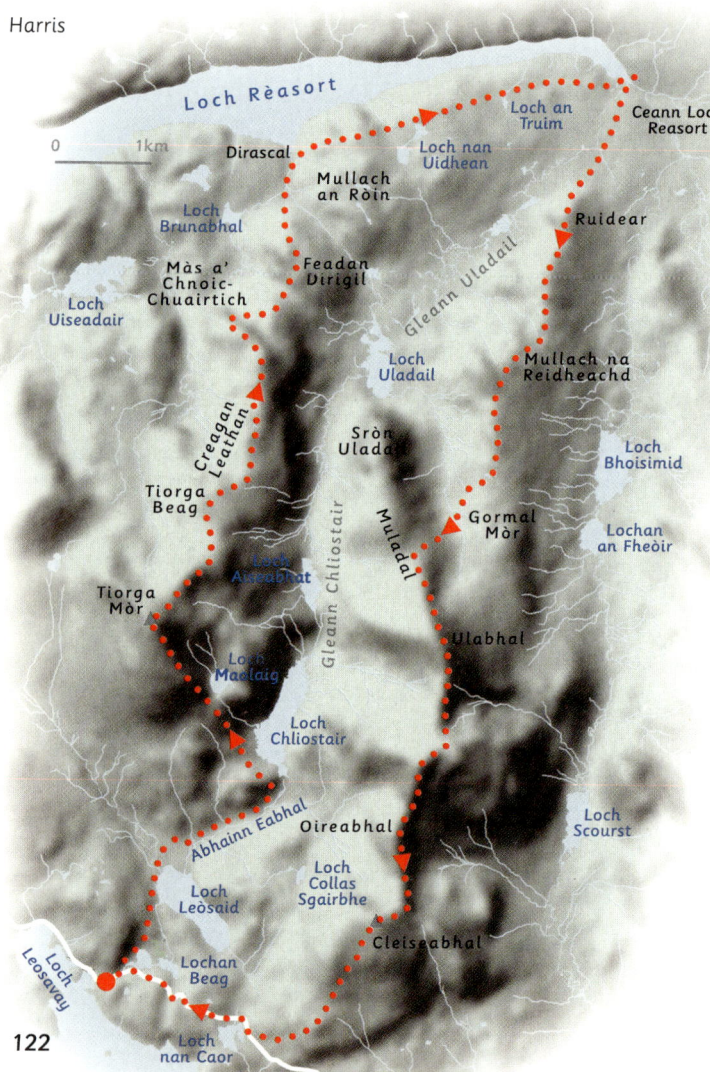

peaks of Ulabhal and Oireabhal, a horseshoe ridge of rocky summits leads up to The Clisham, the highest mountain in the Outer Hebrides.

Descend northeast through rocky terrain, then continue across the narrow grassy ridge to the summit of Tiorga Beag (NB062122). Continue north along the ridge above the rocky cliffs of Creagan Leathan with a good view across the glen to the daunting buttress of Sròn Uladail, lowering over Loch Uladail. Pass a small lochan and continue through rocky terrain to gain the summit of Màs a' Chnoic-Chuairtich (386m), surmounted by a surprisingly substantial cairn.

Descend northwest through rocky terrain, keeping to the ridge for 500m until it is possible to turn east to contour a short way beneath the crags along the steep northeast flank of Màs a' Chnoic-Chuairtich. Once clear of the steep ground, follow the easiest line of descent northeast over rough ground to a bealach, then climb north for 75m to gain the modest summit of Feadan Dìrigil (240m).

There are grand views onto Loch Rèasort and the vast, wild expanse of country beyond. Just over 1km to the north, the next objective should be visible – a collection of ruined shielings by a small inlet at Dirascal. Descend to the north with care – the ground underfoot is very rough and steep in places. On reaching lower ground, follow the watercourses that flow out to Dirascal – the ground is very rough and boggy.

From Dirascal, climb east for 200m and at the 50m contour look for the old track climbing eastwards towards the gap between the high points of Mullach Airispridh and Mullach an Ròin. The climb levels at around 110m, where the old track – metalled with large stones for some of its length – becomes more distinct. Try to keep to the track for the next 2km as it continues east, then northeast across an open expanse of peaty ground, soon passing left of a pair of lochans. The track is eroded in places, but relatively easy to follow until it passes to the left of Loch an Truim where it disappears. Continue northeastwards, soon descending towards the head of Loch Rèasort over rough, eroded ground. Keep to the right of a fenced enclosure and follow the fence to a (locked) estate bothy near the head of the loch and the end of the day's walk.

The old bridge over the Abhainn Mhòr Ceann Reasoirt (NB107172) where it flows into the loch no longer stands; however, as long as the river isn't running high, it's worth crossing to the abandoned metal-roofed house above the old bridge on the far bank, which offers the best ground to pitch your tent with great views down the loch as a bonus.

Day 2

Distance 16km **Total ascent** 1050m **Time** 8 hours 30

Recross the Abhainn Mhòr Ceann Reasoirt and head southwest, initially parallel to the Abhainn Habhsaidh, across eroded peaty ground with dense heather cover. Make for the shoulder of Ruidear and climb up onto the ridge, where the going becomes easier. Follow the ridge – trending south for a while – over a series of rocky knolls marked with stone pile cairns. Cross a bealach and, trending southwest once more, climb a short way to the top of Mullach na Reidheachd at 295m. There are grandstand views southwest onto the impressive overhanging buttress of Sròn Uladail's north face, with Loch Uladail below and Màs a' Chnoic-Chuairtich across the glen to the west. From Mullach na Reidheachd, walk southeast a short way, then descend south along the ridge through rocky and complex terrain to arrive at a lochan perched on a bealach (216m) to the southeast of Sròn Uladail. Begin climbing again, first southwards to Gormal Mòr, then westwards across the head of a stream bed and up on to the north ridge of Ulabhal to the bealach (416m) south of Muladal.

Once on the ridge, turn left and climb south along the steep north ridge of Ulabhal, soon picking your way through and across the broken rock bands higher up to reach the cairn-marked summit at 659m. The summit of Ulabhal provides one of the finest vantage points in all of Harris – on a clear day the views take in a panorama of mountains, lochs, coastline and sea. Continue south down the long narrowing ridge, skirting to the right of a rocky outcrop before arriving at a bealach (564m) with views eastwards into the Cathadail an Ear, which drops dramatically down into Gleann Mhiabhaig. From the bealach, tackle the low crag in front of you straight on, then begin the easy climb southwest to the summit of Oireabhal at 662m.

From the summit of Oireabhal, descend steeply along the southern ridge to a bealach at 460m, then climb a short way up and over the rocky knoll of Bìdigidh (500m). Descend south to another bealach at 425m, then begin the final climb along the ridge which swings to the west before reaching the trig point at the summit of Cleiseabhal (512m). Despite its relatively modest height, Cleiseabhal has a magnificent outlook southeast onto Taransay and along the coast of South Harris to North Uist beyond.

Avoid the steeper ground to the west as you leave the summit by descending the long southwest ridge as if aiming for the island of Sòdhaigh Mòr. Once you reach Mulla Chleiseabhal, swing westwards to meet the B887 near Loch nan Caor. Turn right along the road and follow it for 1.5km back to the start.

Harris

Camping at Ceann Loch Reasort

Harris Hills and Loch Rèasort backpack

Harris

Approaching the summit trig point of Tiorga Mòr

Tiorga Mòr

Distance 12km **Total ascent** 700m
Time 4 hours 30 **Terrain** track road; rugged, rocky mountain terrain; good path through Gleann Leòsaid, boggy in the strath **Map** OS Explorer 456 **Access** bus (W12) to Gleann Chliostair turning (request stop) from Tarbert and Hushinish (Huisinis)

Harris has many fine hills and the elegantly proportioned Tiorga Mòr, standing apart from neighbouring ridges at 679m, is one of the best by any measure.

In part it is the pleasing form, all sweeping lines and cockscomb summit ridge, but its commanding position, dominating the surrounding glens with a vista of hills, coastline and islands near and far, makes Tiorga Mòr a truly standout mountain.

This circular route makes the best of what Tiorga Mòr has to offer, an exhilarating climb, a spectacular summit ridge and not least the series of dramatic reveals as the landscape unfolds around you. There are no difficulties or significant exposure in the ascent and descent, but the southeast and northwest ridges are steep in places, requiring a degree of stamina.

Before reaching Amhuinnsuidhe Castle on the B887 from Tarbert towards Hushinish, turn right along a minor road and follow it for 500m to the turning for a fish farm. Park carefully here. If using the bus, ask to be let down by the Gleann Chliostair turning.

Pass around the gate across the track heading north, continuing along the glen past Loch Leòsaid and over the bridge across the Abhainn Leòsaid. Carry on along the track road, passing the hydropower station, then climbing steadily up the glen. Just before the track passes beneath the pipeline from Loch Chliostair, turn left off the track, climbing northwest on rough ground before gaining a level area just above the loch. Continue, climbing steeply up the southeast ridge of Tiorga Mòr, soon passing above Loch Maolaig nestled in its corrie. This steepest section of the ridge is rocky and rough, but grassy gullies aid progress. The gradient eases as the rocky ground is cleared and a vague path leads towards the rock-crested summit, with its trig point and drystane shelter wall.

There are fine views all around: to the south the whale-backed hills and sparkling beaches of South Harris; east, beyond the peaks of Ulabhal and Oireabhal, a sinuous ridge leads to The Clisham, the highest mountain in the Outer Hebrides; north, the hills of West Lewis and west, down through Glen Cravadale to the Flannan Isles on the horizon. On a clear day you may even see the craggy isles of the St Kilda archipelago on the southwest horizon.

Continue northwest, following a winding path through the rocky pillars and buttresses of the summit ridge. Descend along the widening northwest ridge, making for Bràigh Bheagarais, the bealach lying between Tiorga Mòr and the domed summit of Ceartabhal. From the bealach gradually descend southwestwards using the easiest line to skirt around the north shore of Loch Bràigh Bheagarais.

From the outflow of the loch, descend southwards on the right-hand side of the Abhainn Bràigh Bheagarais, eventually reaching the path climbing through Gleann Leòsaid. Turn left and descend at length along the glen path, crossing a couple of fords on the way down. The path keeps to the left of the Abhainn Leòsaid until it is crossed at a ford by a collection of ruined shielings on reaching the floor of the glen. Once over the burn, carry on through the boggy strath to the right of the burn, recrossing it again to reach the Gleann Chliostair track road once more. Turn right along the road to return to your vehicle or continue to Amhuinnsuidhe Castle to wait for the bus.

Tiorga Mòr

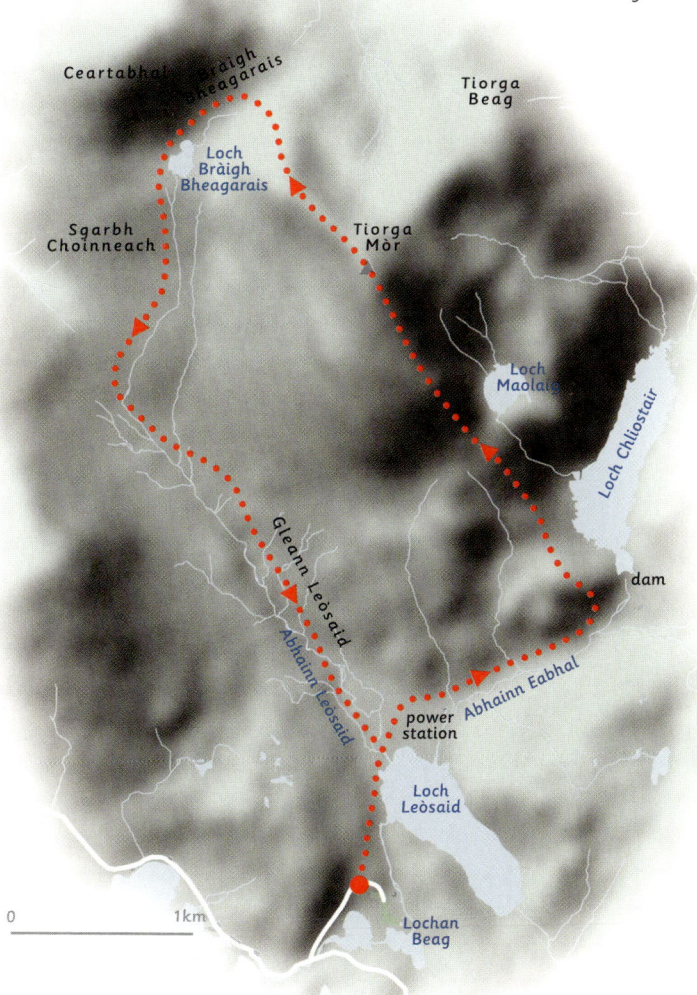

Oireabhal and Huiseabhal Mòr seen from the Isle of Scarp

Huiseabhal Mòr, Oireabhal and Crabhadail

Distance 17.5km **Total ascent** 810m
Time 7 hours **Terrain** track road; good path through Gleann Leòsaid though boggy in the strath; rugged, rocky mountain terrain on the hill; rough and boggy in places when descending to Loch na Cleabhaig and skirting Loch a' Ghlinne **Map** OS Explorer 456
Access bus (W12) to Gleann Chliostair turning (request stop) from Tarbert and Hushinish (Huisinis)

It's fair to say that this route has a bit of everything that you might hope to encounter on a walk in Harris – hills, glens, sandy beaches, sea lochs, freshwater lochs, traces of old settlements, wildlife (good opportunities for spotting eagles and red deer) – and a fair amount of boggy ground as well.

This is a fairly demanding day's walk for most people, but it provokes a sense of accomplishment beyond the effort required, while on a fine day the views from Huiseabhal Mòr, Oireabhal and the bealach above Loch a' Ghlinne are hardly less than astonishing.

There are no real difficulties on this route, though care is definitely required when descending from the bealach between Oireabhal and Huiseabhal Beag towards Loch na Cleabhaig. Some degree of map-reading and navigational competence is also required.

Before reaching Amhuinnsuidhe Castle on the B887 from Tarbert towards Hushinish, turn right along a minor road and follow it for 500m to the turning for a fish farm. Park carefully here. If using the bus, ask to be let down by the Gleann Chliostair turning.

Pass around the gate across the track heading north, continuing along the glen past Loch Leòsaid and over the bridge across the Abhainn Leòsaid. A little beyond the bridge, turn left off the road and head northwest, soon crossing a burn at a silted bend. Continue crosscountry, keeping left of the burn; the strath can be a bit boggy here. Recross the burn where you see

133

a distinct path climbing on the opposite side. Follow the distinct path up through Gleann Leòsaid with Tiorga Mòr dominating its northern flank. The path rises steadily through the glen and eventually you reach the bealach above Glen Cravadale. It's worth descending a short way for the views along Loch a' Ghlinne to Crabhadail – with the Flannan Isles on the horizon – before returning to the bealach.

Turn west here and climb steadily across rough ground to the north of Beidig. Continue climbing more steeply northwest up grassy slopes to reach the summit of Huiseabhal Mòr, which is marked by a small cairn. Although less than 500m high, the summit provides remarkable 360-degree views. From Huiseabhal Mòr, head west across easy ground along the edge of craggy cliffs to reach the summit of Oireabhal. The views from the cliff edge here down to Glen Cravadale, out across Loch Crabhadail and the sands of Tràigh Mheilein on the Sound of Scarp are wonderful. Descend northwest for over 1km to the bealach below the eastern flank of Huiseabhal Beag.

Bear right (NNE) and follow the right-hand side of the Allt a' Ghàrraidh-clach as it descends, steadily at first, into a narrowing gully with traces of trodden path. Cross and recross the burn as and where it aids progress, but keep to the right side further down where the gully opens out, as the burn soon drops into a very narrow rocky gully. Descend with care on the wet, uneven ground, avoiding rocky outcrops. Make for the rear of the estate bothy (private and locked) by the shore of Loch na Cleabhaig and pick up the path to the right, running eastwards. Head up a low rise and then descend past the

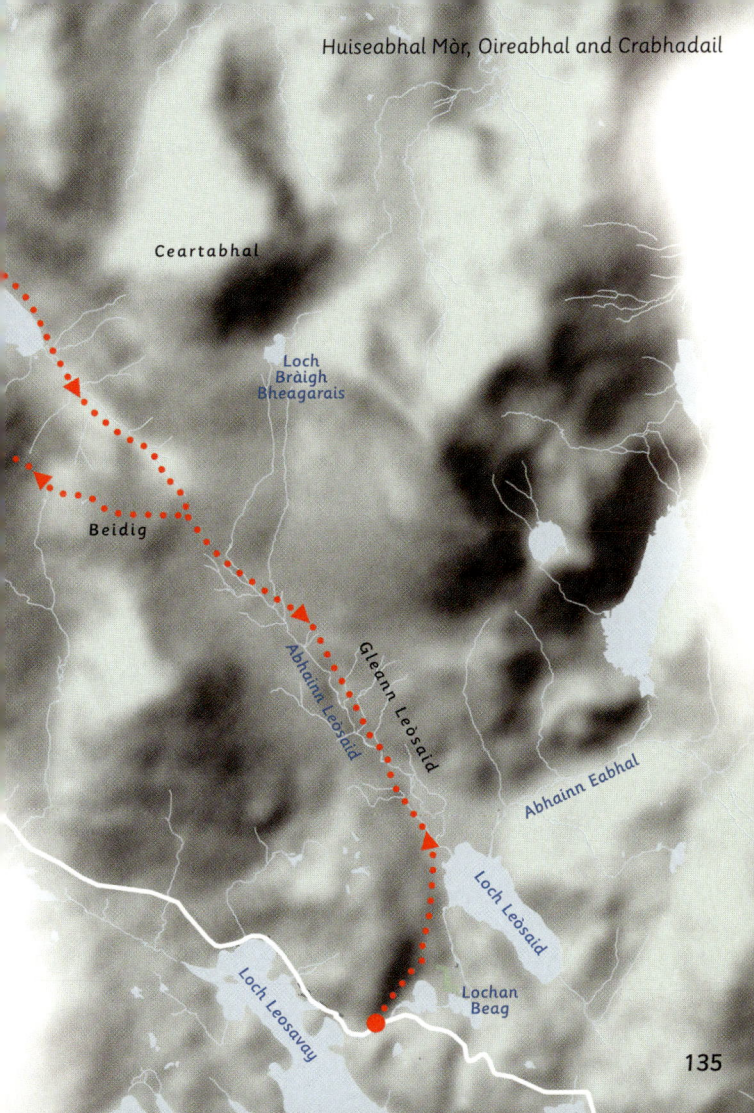

corrugations of ancient lazy beds and the stone piles of ruined shielings to the twin beaches at the head of Loch Crabhadail. This is a fine spot to pause with your flask before continuing on your way.

Follow the beach around to cross the outflow of Loch a' Ghlinne, then continue along a vague path by the eastern shore of the loch. The path becomes more defined near the southern end. Pass some ruined shielings and then climb up through Glen Cravadale, crisscrossing over the Allt a' Ghlinne on the way up. As the gradient eases, you pass a cairn, then another on the flatter ground at the bealach (NB040111). Follow the distinct path down through the glen, crossing the Abhainn Leòsaid by a collection of ruined shielings on reaching the floor of the glen. Once over the burn, continue through the boggy strath to the right of the burn, crossing it again to reach the Gleann Chliostair track road once more. Turn right along the road to return to your vehicle or continue down to Amhuinnsuidhe Castle to wait for the bus.

Old *feannagan* or 'lazy beds' beneath Huiseabhal Beag

Huiseabhal Mòr, Oireabhal and Crabhadail

Beach at the head of Loch Crabhadail

Hushinish and Crabhadail

Distance 10.5km **Total ascent** 375m
Time 4 hours 30 **Terrain** rugged, rocky path, steep near beginning and a little boggy descending to Tràigh Mheilein; sandy beach, dunes and machair
Map OS Explorer 456 **Access** bus (W12) to Hushinish (Huisinis) from Tarbert

The magnificently-situated west coast headland of Huisinis, with its silver sands and flower-speckled machair, is one of the most enchanting corners in all of Harris.

On a fine day, sparkling sea and sand complete the picture of paradise. This route takes in the less-visited but equally splendid beach at Tràigh Mheilein, which looks across the narrow sound to the isle of Scarp, before following the coast around to the beach at the mouth of Glen Cravadale, wedged between saltwater Loch Crabhadail and freshwater Loch a' Ghlinne. The return leg skirts Loch na Cleabhaig before retracing the outward route from the southwestern end of Tràigh Mheilein.

From the parking area by the visitor facilities, head back along the road, cross the cattle grid, then turn left where a wooden signpost indicates Gu Crabhadail. Go through a stock gate and follow the track, soon branching left onto a path indicated by a green marker post. Follow the path parallel to a drystane dyke for 300m before joining another path at a three-way signpost. Bear right (signposted Crabhadail and Tràigh Mheilein) and take the footpath, known locally as the 'Stiamair'.

The path is well made though rocky in places with steep drops at times as it climbs around the rugged coast. Shortly after the top of the climb, branch left off the Crabhadail path onto another trail descending gradually towards the bright white sands of Tràigh Mheilein. This often muddy path leads down to the shore. Make your way along the marvellous beach, enjoying the views across to the old settlement on the east coast of Scarp with its scattering of abandoned roofless stone cottages and several restored holiday homes.

From a peak of 213 in 1881, the population of the Isle of Scarp declined until the last permanent inhabitants quit

Harris

the island in 1971. In July 1934, Scarp was the site of an unsuccessful attempt by German inventor, Gerhard Zucker, to deliver the island's post by means of rocket mail. Though launched successfully, the rocket exploded, destroying or damaging most of its cargo. In 2007, *The Rocket Post*, a heavily fictionalised and romanticised but nonetheless very enjoyable film based on these events, was filmed on Taransay.

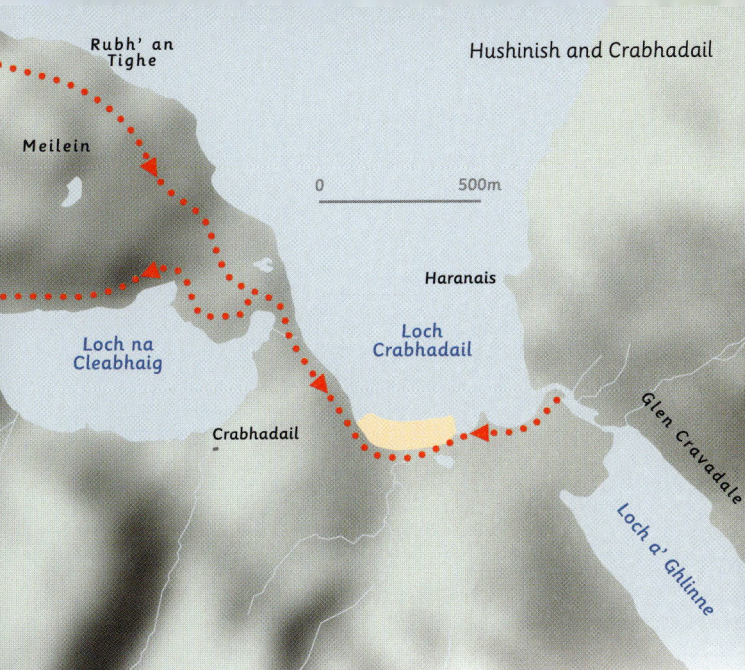

Hushinish and Crabhadail

Where sand gives way to pebbles at the northeastern end of the beach, head up through the dunes, climb through a grassy hollow, then skirt around the eastern flank of Meilein. Contour along before making for the narrow isthmus between the eastern end of Loch na Cleabhaig and Loch Crabhadail. Cross the outflow of the loch, then continue through corrugations of old lazy beds and scattered stones of ruined shielings to the beach at the head of Loch Crabhadail. It's worth continuing a little further to cross the outflow of Loch a' Ghlinne for the view along the loch and glen to the Harris Hills beyond.

Retrace your steps, crossing the outflow of Loch na Cleabhaig, then follow the north shore of the loch to a sandy gap between Meilein and Greascleit. Follow the sheep path through the dunes to the southwestern end of Tràigh Mheilein. Return by the outward route to Hushinish.

Tràigh Mheilein with Scarp across the sound

Hushinish and Crabhadail

Looking west to Scarp from the wild country beneath Taran Mòr

Crabhadail and Taran Mòr backpack

Distance 22km **Total ascent** 1055m
Time 2-3 days **Terrain** mountain and moorland; often pathless, very rough and boggy in places **Map** OS Explorer 456 **Access** bus (W12) to Hushinish (Huisinis) from Tarbert

Taran Mòr is the rocky eminence standing sentinel at the mouth of Atlantic-facing Loch Rèasort, which forms the border between northwest Harris and southwest Lewis. The views from its relatively modest 303m summit over the wild heart of Lewis and Harris are commanding, to say the least. It is, however, a long way from the nearest road and rough, rocky and pathless terrain has to be traversed to get there.

While it is possible – albeit tough going – to walk out to Taran Mòr and back again from Hushinish in a day, the route described here makes the most of some fine, wild country for an all-round superior walk with an overnight camp at Crabhadail. Camping at Crabhadail is no great hardship – it's a great spot to spend a night or two. The walk in from Hushinish laden with camping kit is hard but short-lived. The long second day's walk can be completed without the hindrance of a heavy backpack as you can leave all but day-walk gear in your tent. Spending a second night at Crabhadail is recommended.

The route from Crabhadail heads up Glen Cravadale along the shore of Loch a' Ghlinne and up to the bealach at the head of Gleann Leòsaid before leaving the path to climb to the Bràigh Bheagarais between Ceartabhal and Tiorga Mòr. A rough descent through Gleann Dubh precedes the ascent of Taran Meadhain and Taran Mòr before returning around rough coastline to the beaches at the mouth of Glen Cravadale.

Day 1
Distance 3.5km
Total ascent 185m **Time** 2 hours
From the parking area by the visitor facilities, head back along the road,

Harris

cross the cattle grid, then turn left where a wooden signpost indicates Gu Crabhadail. Go through a stock gate and follow the track, soon branching left onto a path indicated by a green marker post. Follow the path parallel to a drystane dyke for 300m before joining another path at a three-way signpost. Bear right (signposted Crabhadail and Tràigh Mheilein) and take the footpath, known locally as the 'Stiamair'.

The path is well made though rocky in places with steep drops at times as it

Crabhadail and Taran Mòr backpack

climbs around the rugged coast. Shortly after the top of the climb, branch right along the Crabhadail path, soon climbing gently again to the bealach on the south side of Greascleit. Below to the northeast is

147

freshwater Loch na Cleabhaig with saltwater Loch Crabhadail just beyond. Descend the often wet path below the northern cliffs of Huiseabhal Beag, continuing along the southern shore of Loch na Cleabhaig and passing the private estate bothy. Follow the path up a shallow rise, soon looking down across some remarkable corrugations of ancient lazy beds, to the twin beaches at the head of Loch Crabhadail. Continue along the machair above the first beach and cross near the outflow of a burn. There are the sparse remnants of some old shielings here and some shallow scoops in the ground are ideal for pitching a tent.

Day 2

Distance 18.5km **Total ascent** 870m **Time** 8 hours

Follow the beach around to cross the outflow of Loch a' Ghlinne, near the outflow of a burn, then continue along a vague path by the eastern shore of the loch, which is a bit rough and boggy in places. The path becomes more defined near the southern end of the loch. Pass some old shielings and then climb up through Glen Cravadale, criss-crossing over the Allt a' Ghlinne on the way up. As the gradient eases, you pass a cairn, then another on the flatter ground at the bealach (NB040111).

Bear left (northeast) off the path here and begin the steady climb over rough peat-hagged ground, trending north as you gain height and keeping left of the Abhainn Bràigh Bheagarais with the southwest flank of Tiorga Mòr to your right and the south ridge of Ceartabhal straight ahead. Eventually, you reach Loch Bràigh Bheagarais, nestled in the corrie beneath the Bràigh Bheagarais bealach between Ceartabhal and Tiorga Mòr. Continue around the west side of the loch and climb to the bealach with views over Gleann Modail to the wild country around Ceann Loch Reasort.

Descend initially northwards, gradually bearing northwestwards into Gleann Dubh, staying below the crags on Ceartabhal's northeast face. Descend through the rough and often boggy terrain of the glen, crossing the Allt a' Ghlinne Dhuibh and following it down

Crabhadail and Taran Mòr backpack

beneath the crags of An Sith to the open ground at the southwest end of Loch Uiseadair. Cross a burn and make for the channel connecting the smaller loch to the west with the main body of Loch Uiseadair. Cross the channel and continue north across the open ground south of Taran Meadhain. As the ground rises bear northwest to climb to the summit of Taran Meadhain (208m).

Drop southwest, skirting the upper of two lochans before reaching a bealach, then climbing steeply WNW to the summit of Taran Mòr (303m). The views from the summit are incredible. The entire length of Loch Rèasort winds away to Ceann Loch Reasort 8km to the east, while the Uig Hills of southwest Lewis loom to the north. To the southwest lie the Isle of Scarp and the beaches of Crabhadail.

Head initially SSW across the summit plateau, then descend southeastwards, following a broad gully. Swing southwest to drop to the eastern end of the middle of the three lochans collectively known as Lochan na Sgàil and continue along its northern shore and that of the westernmost lochan. Cross the outflow of the westernmost lochan and climb westwards to the obvious gap between boulders and rocky outcrops. Continue to follow vague traces of path with the view opening up ahead straight onto Scarp. Descend a gully on the right-hand side of a small partly-subterranean burn with care. Cross the burn at the obvious point and descend southwestwards with care, avoiding steep ground.

As the gradient eases, take the easiest line southwestwards above the shore, contouring at around 50m or so before dropping to the beach at Haranais. Continue along the coast to Crabhadail, crossing the outflow of Loch a' Ghlinne. Walk around the beach at the head of Loch Crabhadail, cross the outflow of Loch na Cleabhaig and follow its north shore to a sandy gap between Meilein and Greascleit. Follow the sheep path through the dunes to the southwestern end of Tràigh Mheilein. After a gradual climb, join the Crabhadail path and turn right to retrace your steps to Hushinish.

Harris

Crabhadail and Taran Mòr backpack

Scarp seen from the summit of Taran Mòr

Looking down from Àird Uachdarachd to the cliffs at The Gap

St Kilda: walks on Hirta

Distance 8.5km (variant 15km)
Total ascent 720m (variant 1370m)
Time 4 hours (variant 6 hours)
Terrain grassy hills and rugged clifftops; the turf is springy underfoot and generally well-drained, though there is some boggy ground in Gleann Mòr and on the bealach between Mullach Mòr and Conachair **Map** OS Explorer 460
Access several operators offer daytrips sailing to Hirta from Leverburgh, Harris

St Kilda is a group of small islands lying 66km northwest of North Uist. The islands are outliers with cultural links to the Outer Hebrides, but are not part of the archipelago itself.

Hirta is the largest island at roughly 3.5km by 3km at its widest. The island comprises two wide amphitheatre-like bays – one north facing (Glen Bay), the other south facing (Village Bay) – bounded by a ridge of whale-backed hills. The highest point is Conachair (430m); its sheer northern flank is formed by the highest sea cliffs in the British Isles. There are three other islands in the archipelago, Dùn – separated from Hirta by a narrow channel – Soay and Boreray, as well as the immense sea stacks, Stac an Armin (196m) and Stac Lee (172m), which are the highest in the British Isles. Geologically, the islands are remnants of a long-extinct volcano and are largely composed of Tertiary igneous granites and gabbro.

Hirta was inhabited for perhaps 2000 years until 1930, when it was evacuated. The physical remains of this settlement are most apparent on the south side of the island in the street of abandoned houses and the dykes, sheep fanks and cleitan – small stone storage shelters unique to St Kilda – which were often used for storing harvested seabirds. St Kilda is a breeding ground for many important seabird species and has one of the world's largest colonies of northern gannets, numbering around 30,000 pairs. There are significant populations of Leach's petrels, Atlantic puffins and northern fulmars. The St Kilda wren is a subspecies of the Eurasian wren unique to the archipelago and the St Kilda fieldmouse is a

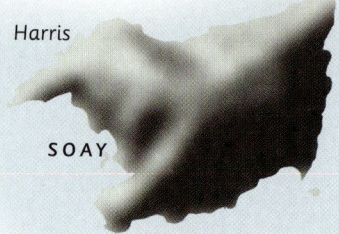
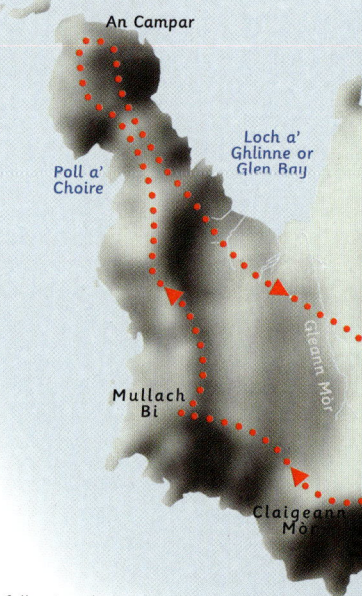

subspecies of woodmouse found only in these islands.

In 1957 St Kilda became a National Nature Reserve with ownership transferred to the National Trust for Scotland. Today, there is a permanent Trust warden on Hirta and during the summer volunteers and professionals work for the Trust, maintaining and restoring the St Kildans' physical legacy. In 1987 St Kilda became a World Heritage Site for its natural history and latterly gained dual WHS status with the inclusion of its cultural heritage.

The sea cliffs at Hirta's north, east and west are extremely high and steep and should be avoided in windy conditions or poor visibility. You should also avoid nesting birds; the island's great skuas, or 'bonxies', will let you know if you're too close by aggressively dive-bombing you.

From the pier, walk up the ramp and turn right past the kirk and then left, following the path up to the 'street' of houses forming the backbone of the abandoned village. Five of the houses have roofs; one hosts a small museum and the others accommodate Trust volunteers. Continue along the street until it peters out, cross the burn at the obvious point, then bear right up towards the gap in the head dyke where the access road passes through.

St Kilda: walks on Hirta

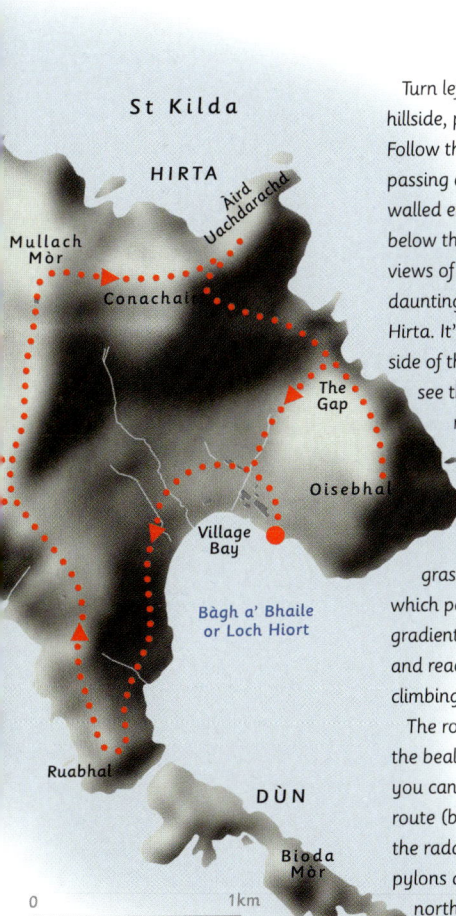

Turn left and contour around the hillside, passing a number of cleitan. Follow the faint path along the low cliffs, passing above several large drystane-walled enclosures. Make for the clifftop below the rocky outcrop on Ruabhal for views of the narrow channel and daunting cliffs separating Dùn from Hirta. It's worth climbing up to the north side of the rocky outcrop on Ruabhal to see the Mistress Stone – a curious rock window capped by a stone slab. There are fine views north and west along the clifftop ridge to Mullach Bi. Continue north, soon climbing a steep grassy slope to join an access road, which passes the radar domes as the gradient eases. Pass a collection of cleits and reach a junction with the road climbing up from the village.

The road winds its way uphill to the bealach at Am Blaid (239m) where you can either follow the longer variant route (below) or carry on up the road to the radar station with its domes and pylons atop Mullach Mòr. From the northernmost tower descend a short way east to the slightly boggy bealach before making the stiff 100m climb to the summit of Conachair (430m), which is marked by a small stone and mortar cairn – an OS trig point lies to the south, 65m below the summit. The views are astounding in every direction – should you be blessed with good visibility.

Descend southeastwards from the summit – taking great care in poor visibility as the north flank of Conachair is the highest sea cliff in the British Isles – on the descent you may find the buckled propellers of a Second World War Bristol Beaufighter that crashed here in 1943.

In good visibility it's worth making a detour along the narrow and steep-sided Àird Uachdarachd promontory jutting northeastwards from the north flank of Conachair. This is a great vantage point for breathtaking views onto the sea cliffs. Follow the clifftops around with care and continue down to The Gap, the low point between Conachair and the neighbouring hill, Oisebhal. To the east of The Gap there is a sheer drop down to the sea.

Climb with care along the clifftop to the summit of Oisebhal (293m) and enjoy more incredible views – this is a great spot for a bird's eye view of the village and its collection of cleits and dykes, as well as across Village Bay to Dùn. When you're done with the views, retrace your steps to The Gap – descending west or southwest from the summit is very steep and awkward. From The Gap, descend southwest towards the village, passing some remarkable drystane-walled sheep fanks. Follow the course of the burn down to the obvious gap in the head dyke which forms the landward perimeter of the village. Hopefully you'll have plenty of time to explore the village before you have to return whence you came.

Variant

Turn left (west) off the road at Am Blaid and cross the bealach to the natural amphitheatre of Gleann Mòr. Follow the faint old track contouring initially westwards around the rim of the glen, passing the rocky eminence of

Claigeann Mòr where the path swings northwest to follow the cliff-top ridge. Pass a collection of cleits and look out for a buttressed rock slab, known as the Lover's Stone, projecting out over the sheer sea cliffs.

According to tradition, the young men of Hirta performed a ritual on the Lover's Stone before they could marry. They would balance on their left foot on the outer edge of the rock with their right foot dangling over the abyss, then bend down and make a fist over their feet. This balancing act demonstrated their agility on the rocks, proving they were able to provide for a family by climbing the cliffs to catch the birds integral to the islanders' diet.

Continue along the ridge with care, watching out for bonxies. Climb up through rocky ground to the high point of Mullach Bi (358m). To the southeast the ridge descends in a series of rocky outcrops over the gap to Dùn with Bioda Mòr as its jagged apex, the whole resembling nothing so much as a dragon's tail. To the northeast, Conachair rises above Mullach Mòr and to the northwest the island of Soay appears beyond the An Campar headland. Continue northwards with care, picking a route down along the rock-studded ridge. At the narrow neck of the headland, bear left to continue around the clifftop. The view back along the cliffs is mightily impressive. Climb up to the high point of An Campar where the view across to Soay and the stacks in the sound is dramatic. Looking back across An Campar, Gleann Mòr is framed to the left by Mullach Mòr and the right by Mullach Bi; some 8km to the northeast lies Boreray and her twin sentinels, Stac Lee and Stac an Armin.

Harris

Index

An Coileach	27
An Reithe	79
An t-Isean	91
Beinn Dhubh	49
Beinn Losgaintir	49
Beinn na Teanga	59
Beinn Sgorabhaig	65
Ceann an Ora	59
Ceapabhal	21
Cleiseabhal	111, 121
Clisham, The	91
Coffin Route, The	39
Crabhadail	133, 139, 145
Eilean Glas	65
Feadan Dìrigil	121
Gatliff Hostel	71, 85
Gillaval Dubh	59
Giolabhal Glas	59
Glean Mhiabhaig	99, 105
Gleann Bhiogadail	99
Gleann Chliostair	111, 115, 121, 129, 133
Gleann Lacasdail	71
Gleann Langadail	99
Gleann Leòsaid	129, 133, 145
Gleann Sgaladail	91
Gleann Uladail	115
Glen Cravadale	133
Grosebay	33
Heileasbhal Mòr	27
Hirta	153
Huiseabhal Mòr	133
Hushinish	139, 145
Lackalee	33, 39
Loch a' Ghlinne	133, 139, 145
Loch Crabhadail	133, 139, 145
Loch Rèasort	121, 145
Loch Seaforth	85, 99
Luskentyre	49, 55
Maaruig	71, 79
Màs a' Chnoic-Chuairtich	121
Meavaig	99, 105
Moilingeanais	71
Muladal	111
Mulla bho Dheas	91
Mulla bho Thuath	91
Mullach an Langa	91
Mullach na Reidheachd	121
Northton	21
Oireabhal (Gleann Chliostair)	111, 121
Oireabhal (Glen Cravadale)	133
Postman's Path	71
Renish Point	13
Rhenigidale	71, 85
Rodel	13, 17
Roineabhal	17
St Clement's Church	13
St Kilda	153
Scalpay, Isle of	65
Scholar's Path, The	33
Seilebost	27, 45
Sgaoth Àird	59
Sgaoth Iosal	59
Skeaudale Horseshoe, The	59
Stràthabhal	79
Stulabhal	105
Taran Mòr	145
Tèileasbhal	105
Tiorga Mòr	121, 129
Tòdun	71, 79
Tràigh Losgaintir	49, 55
Tràigh Rosamol	49, 55
Tràigh Sheileboist	45
Tràigh Mheilein	139, 145
Uisgneabhal Mòr	105
Ulabhal	111, 121
Urgha	71

St Kilda: walks on Hirta

Looking out across Village Bay from the flank of Gonachair